KEEPING BODY
AND SOUL TOGETHER

DENIS LANE

OMF BOOKS

Contents

ISBN 0 85363 144 1

Made in Great Britain
Published by Overseas Missionary Fellowship
Belmont, The Vine, SEVENOAKS, Kent TN13 3TZ
Photoset and printed by Stanley L. Hunt (Printers) Ltd.
Midland Road, Rushden, Northants NN10 9UA

Preface

'THE Church of Jesus Christ is called to preach Good News to the poor, even as its Lord has done in His ministry announcing the Kingdom of God. The churches can not neglect this evangelistic task. Most of the world's people are poor, and they are waiting for a witness to the Gospel that will really be Good News. . . . The mission which is conscious of the kingdom will be concerned for liberation, not oppression; justice, not exploitation; fullness, not deprivation; freedom, not slavery; health, not disease; life not death. No matter how the poor may be identified, this mission is for them.'

So runs Section 1, 16 of the report of the 1980 Melbourne Conference of the Commission on World Mission of the World Council of Churches.

'We have become so accustomed to the concept of social action as social engineering or as the application of political pressure in the name of Christ that we are not quite prepared to see that bringing men to a saving relationship to God in Christ is itself action that aims at the transformation of all other relationships. It is social action.'

So writes Dr William J Richardson of Northwest Christian College, Eugene, Oregon, USA in 'Social Action vs Evangelism' (William Carey Library).

One says social action is evangelism. The other says evangelism is social action. So the issue burns on and the Christian world divides. The issue is vital, both for the truth of God in a secular world and for the meeting of the screaming needs of the suffering silent majority in two-thirds of the world. Neither the WCC nor Dr Richardson would feel that they are neglecting the other half of the equation.

Yet the WCC would probably say that Dr Richardson's social action is inadequate, not touching the evil structures from which men and women need to be 'saved'. Dr Richardson probably feels that the WCC's evangelism is inadequate, not dealing with man's fundamental and primary need of reconciliation with God through the proclamation of the Good News of Jesus Christ. Both would say that they believe in evangelism *and* social action. The problem is, which comes first?

The Lausanne Covenant put the balance very well,

'Although reconciliation with man is not reconciliation with God, nor is social action evangelism, nor is political liberation salvation, nevertheless we affirm that evangelism and socio-political involvement are both part of our Christian duty.'

This book does not pretend to be a continuation of the discussion about which comes first. It is not a contribution to theoretical debate of principles, vital as such dialogue may be. Rather, it sets out to show how one missionary society has faced the issues in different countries of East Asia at a practical level. We have often been asked in recent years why we do not use more of the money that is abundantly available from relief and social action agencies. Are we not concerned for the physical needs of the people to whom we go?

I have sought to show first of all the principles which motivate our thinking on social action, and then to illustrate from real-life situations how these principles have led us to quite widespread involvement in the needs of the whole person. *Denis Lane*

1 Preaching and Serving

No generation has ever faced world needs on the scale that we face them today. Certainly, no generation has known so much about so many needs in so many places as we do. The proliferation of technology and the explosion of population communicates the plight of a greater number of people than ever before, and we are tempted to try to meet all the needs everywhere at once. But we are not God. He knows that more people are alive today than at any period in man's history, and He also knows their needs from the oldest to the youngest. He alone has the capacity to take in those needs and to deploy His infinite resources to meet them. We must not try to play God. We do have a part to play, however, and He can and will show us what that part is. Finding it out is our problem, and in order to do so we need to arrive at certain principles on which we can depend, and to take into account certain factors that apply to us and may not necessarily apply to others. As a missionary society we seek to act as part of God's family and Christ's Body, and there are certain principles and factors on which we feel we should base our involvement in the wider needs of the whole man today. I invite you to consider them with me and, if you share our outlook, to participate with us in the small contribution we can make to a suffering world. The missionary force is but the tip of the iceberg. Behind it must stand an army of intercessors and fellow workers who make the missionaries' involvement both possible and effective.

First Principle:
Social and spiritual needs do not necessarily conflict

Human need is human need, of whatever kind. Scripturally, spiritual and social need are as close as belief and life, faith and works, body and soul, hand and glove. Polarization of needs multiplies problems. God is the God of the whole of life, and in teaching us that 'daily bread' is a legitimate and necessary subject for prayer, the Lord joined the spiritual and the physical together. Therefore, to oversimplify by polarizing issues only complicates them. What we do have to grapple with are the relative priorities for a limited number of people facing an unlimited sea of need. Many people in Asia face not one network of problems, but a multiple network of them. They are often caught up in a tangle of debt, a world of injustice, a cauldron of corruption, the daily drag of sub-standard health, a pattern of poverty, and a mind set that inhibits action. They probably believe that their fate is pre-determined anyway, whether by the will of God or the inevitable result of past incarnations. Faced with the question of what to tackle first, we have to be clear in our sense of priorities for our own particular contribution, recognizing that a person who is set free in one area often finds that something else has laid its tentacles upon him, so that he is like a swimmer escaping from an octopus.

Sometimes priorities lie clearly to view, as in the emergency situations which erupt in different places at different times. Desperate though those emergencies may be, in one sense they are simpler to deal with. A starving person clearly needs food before anything else; a refugee needs a home. However, once the emergency has been dealt with, the situation reverts to 'normal' and a multitude of new problems rear their head. Then the choice of priorities again becomes difficult.

8

Second Principle:
Changing the structures of society does not meet the needs of the Whole Man

Some of our 'Liberation Theology' friends would have us believe that the primary danger menacing the life and welfare of a large proportion of the world's population lies in the evil social structures that oppress them. I would agree that 'salvation' in a biblical sense involves liberating man from the dangers menacing his life, and setting him free to live life to the full. I would agree too that many present day human structures are evil or carry evil consequences. On the other hand, to ignore the danger to life and welfare posed by man's alienation from God, and not to see that that alienation results in a basic self-centredness which leads to the evil structures, is to miss the root cause of the disease. Neither capitalism nor communism have particularly good records in meeting the deepest needs of the people who live under their systems. We have seen many structures swept away in revolutions over the last thirty years, but very few better societies have emerged as a result. Indeed, the history of the past thirty years would surely make us hesitate to overturn existing structures in a violently radical sense, without first asking ourselves whether what is to follow is going to be any better. To imagine that all that is needed is a change of system is not only to oversimplify the issue but to be incredibly naîve.

The Christian diagnosis takes full account of human sin and self-centredness. It sees man subject to his environment in human society organized as though God did not exist, a slave to his own selfish desires, and controlled by forces much bigger than he is. In the words of older terminology, the Christian diagnosis sees man as bound by the world, the flesh and the devil. We do not see this as antiquated dogma, but as a 'true' description of the ultimate reality of things. In that context, the liberating power of the life, death, and resurrection of Jesus Christ do not rank as items of Christian propaganda, but as events of history with the explosive power to shatter the chains that bind men and women. A renewed relationship with God then sets them free to live life as it was meant to be lived, as creatures before their Creator. The view that a change in the structures of society is all that is needed is not too radical; rather it is not radical enough. 'Radical' means to go to the roots of something, and changing the structures of society simply leaves the roots untouched.

Third Principle:
The Gospel does have and must have social effects

We cannot take this for granted. Salvation must clear the spiritual dangers menacing the life and welfare of men and women. But the other dangers that menace their lives and welfare are just as real. Poverty, malnutrition and injustice all cripple people's ability to live the life God intended them to. Therefore Christians and missions must not pretend that in introducing people to new life in Jesus Christ we have automatically solved their problems. They have to be taught to understand the implications of their new belief, and some of those implications are social. Unfortunately, many of our Western churches have never gone very far in this, so that congregations of believers can be surrounded by appalling social needs without ever thinking that the Gospel calls them to act to alleviate them. We even have the spectacle of people professing the Christian faith in church on Sunday and actively participating in an unjust situation through the week, when they may be in a position to change or at least to challenge the evil structure.

Paul, writing to the Ephesians, told the thief not to steal any more, but rather to 'work, doing something useful with his own hands, that he may have something to share with those in need' (Ephesians 4.28). The apostle did not take it for granted that any believer who had been a thief would automatically realize that stealing was wrong and should be abandoned. So, while the Gospel should have and does have special effects, they cannot be taken for granted: people have to be made alert both to the needs and to what can be done about them.

Therefore, while the basic need of men and women is reconciliation to God and new birth through the Spirit of God, the further implication of that new birth in love expressed to our neighbour is not an optional extra to be added by those with an interest in social affairs, but part of the warp and woof of Christian living. Christ is not only made to us justification, but also sanctification (1 Corinthians 1.30), and we cannot have one without the other. The Christ cannot be divided. Therefore if there are no effects in the individual life of the believer, and if there are no visible effects in his or her relationships and attitudes to society around, we may legitimately question the depth and reality of his or her experience of reconciliation with God.

At this point, let me illustrate from some examples how the Gospel, rightly understood and implemented, does go to the root of many problems. One area of concern for people today is the dignity and worth of the individual person. Pressured by mass media, and conscious of being a tiny creature in the midst of millions of others, modern man finds it hard to believe he has any lasting worth. Facing the impersonal bureaucracy of the State machine, he feels like a statistic on a computer. Strange to say, some of the systems of

11

government founded most firmly on humanistic principles tend to reinforce these feelings most strongly. When the dominant belief is that human nature is just a part of the whole structure of the universe, and that our greatest hope is to be reabsorbed into the fathomless sea of total existence, then in practice the individual counts for less. The Christian basis for human dignity and worth is the fact of creation and the purchase price of redemption. If God loved us enough to make us all different, and Christ died to save us, then we are invested with a worth beyond ourselves which is inherent in the very nature of reality. Nowhere is this seen more clearly than in the realm of medical ethics.

A missionary surgeon teaching a group of medical students in an Asian country stood by a hospital bed. 'Who is the most important person in this hospital?' he asked. Answers varied from the chief surgeon to the chairman of the board, and various other prominent personalities. When in the end the surgeon pointed to the patient, he was met with astonishment and disbelief. To reckon one individual as important, especially when he might well be a person low down in the social scale, was quite beyond their comprehension. So, many nurses consider themselves like civil servants, and if a task is below their estimate of their proper role they will have nothing to do with it. Many of the remaining standards of medical ethics in our Western countries derive in origin from a Christian base that is fast disappearing. How long will the standards themselves remain? Some people assure me that they are in fact disappearing already.

Another area where Christian truth can make a big difference is when it cuts at the root of a fatalism which passively accepts every evil as unavoidable. We believe that God is sovereign, but we do not believe in a blind fatalism or determinism. Man is held responsible for his actions and will one day be called to account. Therefore he need not and indeed must not sit down under a situation and ascribe it to the will of God or the result of his past actions in this or some other life. When floods threatened Manorom Hospital in Thailand a few years ago, lorry loads of earth were brought in to build up the dykes confining the river and to fight the water that was rising inch by inch. When in the end the waters receded, not only the hospital had been saved but also acre upon acre of rice fields belonging to local farmers. They would have found it hard to interfere with nature in this way, accepting the flooding as part of their inevitable fate.

We may find this difficult to understand, but not long ago I heard a message on Psalm 19 given by a Malaysian Christian. He waxed quite lyrical about the glory of God in creation, and not least in the stars. Then he explained that many Asian people find it hard to appreciate nature in the sense, for instance, of admiring a sunset. This is because in several Asian religions man is not set over nature in the divine order of creation, as a steward of God's resources. Rather, he is only a part of the natural scene, and his future hope centres upon being re-absorbed into the whole of which he is a part. Therefore he views nature differently. Rather than interfering with nature or changing its course in any way, his role is to submit to natural forces however devastating, and passively to endure whatever they bring. This outlook develops a longsuffering patience completely foreign to the West, but it also hinders the control of natural forces for the benefit of the community. Westerners have interfered in nature too much and often unwisely, and that is the other extreme.

A third example of the difference made by Christian belief when carried into life is the creation of a caring community. In many ways Asian societies have a far greater community spirit than Western ones, but usually that spirit depends upon family, clan, or tribal relationship. Too often the church fails to demonstrate community life and concern. Yet when a church lives out the truth of the Body of Christ, a fresh dimension comes into play. So in the middle of an Akha village in Thailand stands a rough bamboo structure where the Christian community stores ten percent of all its rice harvest. Then, when a family in another village believes and as a consequence is thrown out of their home, there is rice available in the Christian village to feed them until their first harvest in the new place is reaped.

On one occasion a fairly new church faced a problem about where they could bury their dead. The local facilities were denied them, and the only place where temporary burial for three years was possible was some way away in a Roman Catholic cemetery. Because of the high water level and the need to move the coffin within three years, it had to be made of very strong wood and lined with lead. The result was somewhat heavy! At the time of the funeral the rain bucketed down and the roads were terrible. Not far out of town, buses slewed across the road barred their progress. People in the locality found the plight of these Christians something of an entertainment. Then the whole Christian group gathered round the truck on which the coffin had been placed, and with the help of a tractor heaved and pushed the truck off the road, across the fields past the buses, and up on to the road again. Everyone, of course, was liberally coated with mud. But the comments that then began to be made by some of the bystanders were very interesting. Their amusement had changed to appreciation as they realized, 'We would never have helped each other in circumstances like that. There must be something in this Christianity if it makes people work together in this way.'

The Gospel does have and must have social effects, but they cannot be taken for granted. Too often evangelical Christians have assumed that faith leads to works, without teaching either their necessity or the kind of works that might be appropriate. So nothing happens. Another factor is that many of the intractable problems of societies which have deeply entrenched ways of doing things demand deep thinking, constant trial and error and maturity in experience if they are to be tackled. The newly emerging church may not have the maturity, the qualified personnel, or the vision to do this, yet it does have the experience of living within the society for many years, and the greatness of the problem is no excuse for not teaching the need to tackle it.

Fourth Principle:
Money is a dangerous commodity

Why does the OMF use comparatively little money in relief operations? One reason is a geographical one. Most of the countries of East Asia have fruitful soil and plenty of rain — sometimes too much — which means they are not subject to some of the devastations of drought and flood that afflict countries like India and Bangladesh. Typhoons wreak their havoc, in the Philippines especially, but only in a limited area. Not at present being overpopulated to the extent of India, for example, East Asian countries do not face quite the same depths of poverty. Plenty of people are poor, grindingly so, but not to the point of emergency. Therefore, until the flood of Indo-Chinese refugees burst out, the number of emergency situations demanding large scale relief was few compared with Africa and many other parts of the world.

The real problems of East Asian poverty cannot be met by an infusion of money here and there. They are tied to the very fabric of society which, humanly speaking, we are powerless to touch, and in which the indiscriminate use of money raises more problems than it solves. Much more effective is the enabling of people to improve their own lot by simple technology already available to them on the local scene. Hence the scheme (detailed later) by which the Akha people have been helped to develop settled paddy fields, instead of their traditional system of slashing and burning the countryside and moving on when the soil is worked out. The financial cost of such a scheme is minimal.

A further problem for the missionary is that, if financial help is allied to the proclaiming of the Gospel, professions of belief for the wrong reasons are only too possible. In Muslim countries such help is viewed as spiritual bribery; and rather than the Christian contribution being seen as assisting the land, it may well be seen as undermining their religious background. Again, when large sums of money are involved there can easily be competition for administering it and sometimes an unhealthy desire to use it in ways that may not be the best for the community. We have ourselves experienced some of these complications, to our cost.

Not that OMF does not use finance in social action. Three hospitals in Thailand, while largely running on their own income, need capital expenditure. The alcoholics rehabilitation centre in Japan had to be built, and the Mangyan Development Programme in the Philippines has to be maintained for the duration of its launching. Groups like TEAR Fund in Britain, the Blue Cross in Switzerland and the German Agency have been most generous in their assistance. We do not use more money, partly because we want our assistance to be appropriate to the resources and needs of the people, and partly because there are often groups within the country concerned that specialize in this kind of ministry and it is better to leave them to their speciality.

Fifth Principle:
As missionaries we are guests in the countries in which we work

We are not insiders, but we try to be sympathetic outsiders. We must therefore be careful that our actions are not unnecessarily misunderstood. I have already mentioned the danger of appearing to offer spiritual bribery, and the problem of false belief for the wrong reasons. As outsiders to the culture we cannot always discern clearly what is a true or false profession of faith. Jesus Himself knew the dangers involved in providing bread for five thousand hungry hearers. He told them quite plainly, 'I tell you the truth, you are looking for me, not because you saw miraculous signs, but because you ate the loaves and had your fill.' If Jesus could not avoid some people following Him for the wrong reasons, we are unlikely to succeed. We do of course still have to try. Jesus did feed them.

Yet many social issues spill over into the political realm, and it is at this point that a foreign missionary must be very careful. We are not there to right the political wrongs of someone else's country. After all, we have not succeeded very well in dealing with our own. If we do stray into the political realm we are likely to find ourselves on the next plane home, for Asian governments have enough home-bred subversives to cope with, without importing others in the name of religion. Here the missionary may face a host of agonies. He may feel that he is a citizen of a country which is bolstering a corrupt regime somewhere; yet at the same time he may be aware that the succeeding regime could well be a lot worse. Few people could support the Cambodian government with too much enthusiasm before the fall of that country, but the regime that followed was a nightmare in comparison. Again, the missionary is aware that he is part of the affluent majority, and not know how to cope with this.

As I view this complex issue, two things seem clear. One is that we must know our facts and be sympathetically understanding, both of the efforts that governments make to improve conditions and of the enormous odds stacked against them. Corruption, for example, is easier to see than to solve, especially when it is built into the very fabric of society from the top to the bottom. If policemen do not get paid a living wage because the country cannot afford it, how can they live without making something on the side? We can easily raise our voices to condemn without knowing what we would do if we were faced with the same problem. Then we have to look at the sheer scale of the problems. When the population of a country has doubled or even nearly tripled in the last thirty years, it has little foreign exchange, no resources of oil and comparatively little industry, and is split into several ethnic and linguistic groups, how do the leaders hold everything together and improve the overall standard of living? A government that makes any progress in such a context deserves sympathetic understanding at least. We need, as James tells us, to be swift to hear and slow to speak. In the modern world we tend rather to be quick to speak and slow to sympathize, and Christians can easily follow the way of the world. Paul taught us to pray for those in authority, not pelt them with half-digested criticisms. That does not mean that we have to close our eyes to the injustices of power structures, or to the concentration of wealth in the hands of the few. But we do need to remember that every leader is in some ways a prisoner in his own political and economic environment.

The second vital principle is that challenging social ills and changing unjust structures must be the task of national Christian leaders rather than of missionaries. Only the insider can challenge the wrongs within a culture adequately, and only he has the equipment and qualifications to change it. What we can and must do as sympathetic outsiders is to teach the biblical principles which govern social relations, and encourage national believers to apply them to their own situations. We are not citizens to meddle politically, but we can teach the ground rules of the kingdom of God. Unfortunately, we have been so weak in applying scriptural principles to our own cultures for so long, that much of the time we are unaware of what those principles are. We need to do our homework too.

* * * * *

These then are some of the main principles on which we as a Fellowship base our approach to social action. We see our primary calling and commission from God as the preaching of the Gospel of our Lord Jesus Christ. We do not believe that He or the Gospel are irrelevant to social needs, but we do believe that it is men and women who must be changed, and not their circumstances alone. We see our calling as the teaching of the Gospel with all its implications for the life of the community.

The preaching of the Gospel is rather like peeling an onion — when we start the process we start something that has no end. We remove one layer and another appears beneath. In the same way, we preach the Gospel and another need becomes clear. Deal with that and yet another problem surfaces. We cannot ignore the subsequent problems and content ourselves with the first layer. But we do have to begin with the first layer, and for us that is the preaching of the Gospel. Peeling an onion produces tears. So does preaching the Gospel and social action. Opening a hospital is a work of joy, but closing one is an agony of tension. Healing leprosy rejoices the heart, but rehabilitating patients in an un-welcoming society stretches the patience. The easiest thing would be to opt out entirely — no onion, no tears. But then the meal would be tasteless.

19

So let me share with you some of the layers that have been revealed as we have preached the Gospel in different countries in East Asia. Our part is only a tiny one, but it is the one God has given us to play, and Jesus said that fulfilling the work God has given us to do is the most rewarding of occupations.

2 Tribal Trauma

'As usual the whites introduced diseases to the nationals.' A small comment which ended a television review of a film about the death of the five missionaries to the Auca in South America in 1956; but it contains a weight of derogatory overtones. Pictures spring to mind of idyllic societies living close to nature and enjoying simple life styles free from the complications and corruptions of western society. Into these ideal communities thrust the big-nosed intruders to force their views on the gullible people, destroying their beautiful culture and in the process bringing new diseases into their healthy havens. Yes, missions have had their ham-fisted, culturally insensitive practitioners. But the realities are not so ideal or so simple as people would like to believe.

For one thing, very few tribal societies can be described in these utopian terms. They have many commendable characteristics, but they also have their share of sin. Fear often dominates their whole outlook — fear of spirits, fear of other groups and fear of their environment. Driven to live in inaccessible and unproductive regions, not by missionaries but by exploitation and expulsion from their lands, they have come to terms with often inhospitable environments. That does not necessarily mean that if they had a choice they would want to continue as they are. On the very same evening when the programme mentioned above was shown, another portrayed a 'megalithic society' in Asia. The commentary was punctuated by references to slaves or enemies sacrificed in former days when houses were built or dedicated, and the need for blood-shedding at every turn. Fortunately their culture has changed and the cameramen came back with their heads still on shoulders.

The fact is that cultures do and will change, and a missionary is only one kind of agent in the field. The Manobo people of Mindanao in the Philippines had never had to handle money until recently. They did not need it in their culture. Then the loggers came, slicing swathes of brown track through the lush forests. They needed help to move the trees and load them on to trucks, and they paid in cash. What is the use of money, though, if you do not know what to spend it on? Cheap rum proved attractive and readily available to the Manobo, with a noticeable and disturbing effect on their culture. Missionaries then came in along the same brown tracks, but their impact on the culture went in a different direction. Cultures can and do change, but not all change is bad. As responsible agents of change, we missionaries have to ensure that as far as possible the changes we cause are not only in the right direction, but able to be absorbed by the changing society.

In North Thailand pressures on all the tribal groups have increased dramatically in recent years. For one thing the population has exploded: both because better health brings less infant mortality and so more mouths to feed, and also because of increasing numbers of people moving across from both Burma and Laos to escape political unrest. More people need more food and more land. Then the Northern Thai farmers have come in on the act. Needing more land for more food for their own population, they have gradually pushed further and further into the mountains. Finally the government, with increasing knowledge of the environment and increasing awareness of the harm done by indis- criminate destruction of upland forests, has brought in restrictions and designated some areas as forest reserves. For people whose customary method of farming is to slash down the jungle, burn it off and then after a few crops repeat the process elsewhere, the combination of these forces has been traumatic in the extreme.

The present crisis is at the same time economic, cultural and social. As economic conditions deteriorate, extended families break down and so cultural patterns must change. When a people begin to lose their identity they feel a sense of loss, but are not always capable of understanding what is happening to them and why. Then the missionary who has learnt their language and something of their culture can come alongside, help them to understand, and maybe interpret to them what is happening. He can act as a resource person, helping to inform tribal people of existing government projects, and sometimes too as a liaison between tribal groups and the authorities.

By the early 1970s churches had emerged among the Akha, Lisu, Yao, Hmong and Pwo Karen tribes, and Christian communities as well as others needed to know how to cope with change. In 1974, because of the pressing nature of the problems, OMF's North Thailand field appointed Freddie Gasser, a Swiss agricultural missionary, as field agriculturalist working alongside the local missionaries and tribal leaders. Freddie's task was to help tribal people learn to grow new crops, raise new kinds of livestock, use their land more effectively, develop irrigation for rice fields and find markets for their produce.

Freddie and his wife Ruth are still missionaries even though their work is mainly agricultural. They still engage in language study, for in North Thailand every missionary must first learn standard Thai, then adapt somewhat to the linguistic differences of Northern Thai and then learn a tribal language. The Gassers are learning Akha, and this will extend their usefulness beyond agricultural instruction to teaching in leadership conferences and short-term Bible schools, for example. Integration between spiritual and farming instruction underlines the wholeness of man and his needs.

One of the earliest efforts of the programme involved

bringing a dozen young people from Switzerland to share in a work camp. Preparations to feed a group like that for six weeks in a mountain situation, without imposing strain on the tribal economy, meant widening a trail enough to take a motor bike for bringing in supplies, as well as planting vegetables in time to be able to pick them when the camp was on. At first the Akha people could not believe that anyone could care about them this much, and not until the Swiss young people appeared up the trail were they really convinced they would come. But come they did, with willing hands and singing voices. During the day tribesmen and young Swiss laboured together making paddy fields alongside a mountain brook. In the evenings around the fire the two mountain peoples sang songs to each other in their own language, and the warmth of the fire reflected the warmth of fellowship in hearts at one in Christ.

A second camp showed the Akha how to prevent loss of topsoil on a hillside by terracing, and a third went to the Pwo Karen tribe. The first Pwo Karen Christian needed help to improve his hill fields, and as the young people began to get their hands dirty in his field, his heart was impressed. Most Asian cultures have no great respect for the person who works with his hands; but people began to watch, and then other Christians started to see new meaning in the Lord's command to 'Subdue the earth. I have given it to you for raising food' (Genesis 1.28). New methods came in and new benefits resulted.

Because the Gospel had removed the binding fear of the spirits, one Pwo Karen Christian dared to plant a field regarded by his unbelieving neighbours as spirit-haunted. They would not dare to touch it, but he reaped a rich harvest that year. Yet here too there was no separation between the spiritual and the practical. The missionaries stood with this man in a prayer battle against what he and they knew to be real spiritual forces. So one missionary prayed and taught the spiritual warfare, and another worked and taught soils and seeds, and both contributed to a harvest where before there was nothing but weeds.

Freddie and Ruth Gasser now live in the Akha Christian village known as Elephant Valley. It gets its name from the mountain at the head of the valley, which looks just like the outline of the beast known so well in the timber camps of the north. As well as language study, Freddie works alongside key people in the village. At first he helped the headman and taught him to terrace fields; later he went on to rotation of crops and how to get the best out of the land. He introduced simple equipment such as a home-made harness, so now the people are learning to control horses and fasten them to simple carts, ploughs and harrows, also home-made. Previously the Akha could not use the same land again and again because the tough cogan grass soon covered the fallow field and defied all attempts to remove it. But now a simple plough allows for deeper action and more efficient use of the land.

A Christian community helps villagers to work together. In Elephant Valley, the headman and three daring innovators are slowly working more and more together to produce better results. At first the accomplishment may not seem to match the labour, but one successful harvest trumpets across the hillsides that here is something better. Just as the church is a struggling outpost of a new humanity, so a clean ploughed field stands out in contrast to a knotted jungle or weed-plagued area around.

Heartaches there are in plenty. The best ploughed field needs rain in the right amount at the right time. Blight and rats attack anyone's fields. Not every Christian learns quickly, and by no means all want to change age-old habits. People are still people, even with the grace of God in their hearts.

'Where are you going?' Freddie asked A baw li one day.

'I go to the fields,' he replied.

'What are you going to do there?'

'I'm going to thresh out my rice.'

'What will be your yield this year?'

'I should think about 90 Bip' (about 12 sacks).

'Will that be sufficient for you, your wife and your children to have enough to eat through the coming year?'

'No, it is not enough, it will do for about nine months.'

'What about the remaining three months?'

'I will have to buy some.'

'In that case I advise you to buy right now,' Freddie told him. 'At this time of the year the rice is cheaper. In about two or three months' time it will be much more expensive to buy the same amount.'

'I can't think about that yet. I guess the Lord can give me the money in small or big amounts. . . .'

A baw li moved away towards his field, and Freddie went back thoughtfully to his work. In a sense what A baw li had just said was quite true: the Lord is able to help in small or big amounts; He can provide, whether the market price is high or low. But what if there is laziness involved? Does God even out all irregularities in life, even though they may be caused by carelessness or negligence? Is poverty a social or a spiritual problem?

Of the thirty Christian families of Elephant Valley, most have been Christians for nearly ten years, although others only turned away from idols and spirits fairly recently. Those who are Christians of long standing have experienced the Lord's goodness in many ways. For example, in 1976 there was a village fire, in which all their goods, possessions and rice were completely destroyed. At that time they learned the art of receiving thankfully, as the Lord prompted many Thai and western Christians to help meet their needs, especially in overcoming the shortage of rice. But several years later, some are still content to receive; one of the main

26

lessons they need to learn is that privilege carries responsibility and eating means working. The families which were still not producing their full share ate as much as the others! If there is not enough rice in the granaries or funds are lacking, they put a strain on the headman by expecting him to provide for them. Sometimes the problem arises through carelessness, as with A baw li, who will be in need in nine months' time. There are at least five other Christian families who will be short. They have to learn that Christianity and bread-winning go together, and the Gassers try to show this partly by setting up a demonstration layout for fields, and partly by teaching the people practical skills. Alongside the teaching of the practical went teaching of the spiritual principles that require a Christian to work for his living and to carry his belief into the fields along with his hoe.

After the rice harvest is in, Akha men tend to hang around the village, day-dreaming or sleeping, or to go hunting for fun, while in many a family there are big needs to be met. Even Christians of long standing cannot see beyond their own small corner — Elephant Valley seems to them the beginning and the end of the world. Freddie and Ruth look forward to the time when the love of Akha Christians is not limited to the small circle of the Elephant Valley church, while many Akha in other villages are waiting to be taught and evangelised.

Missionaries such as the Gassers feel that the Lord has called them to show in a practical way what the apostle Paul taught in Ephesians, 'The man who used to rob (and beg) must stop it and begin using these hands of his to earn an honest living for himself and to be able to help the needy and the poor.'

3 Bridges of Change

THE first time I visited the tribal peoples of North
Thailand we walked for a time across dry rice fields with
the sun pouring fiery heat upon us from above. So I was
glad when we began to move into the hills, and the ever-
increasing number of trees threw welcome shade across
our path. Then we came to a river, and my delight
disappeared in an instant. Across the river and right in
our path swayed the most rickety bridge I had ever seen.
I have never been one for heights at the best of times,
and while the prospect of falling twenty feet into a
swirling stream may be infinitely preferable to that of
dropping on to concrete, I had no real wish to do either.
The bridge consisted of a few bamboo poles, each
moving at the slightest touch and seemingly indepen-
dent of all the others, with one slender rattan rope at the
side. We had been warned years before that missionaries
must be expected to preach, pray or die at a moment's
notice. I had no one to preach to, but I certainly prayed
and fervently hoped that I might be spared the last part.

My agony lasted only a few moments and then we were
over the bridge and moving along the trail. But this
experience was a helpful reminder to me that many of
our tribal brothers and sisters face far worse bridges,
stretching into the foreseeable future and causing them
quite as much anxiety, or even more. For them to cross
such a physical obstacle would be the work of a moment
and the habit of a lifetime. But to cross the bridges of
change across their path is a different matter, and we
have a responsibility to help them. What are some of
their problems?

While on a visit to another tribe, I had as my com-
panion Theo Welch, then an OMF missionary teaching
surgery in the hospital in Chiengmai. We climbed high

into the hills, panting to keep up with Leona Bair, another missionary who lived in Lime Village, our destination. Eight hours of walking, climbing and slithering brought us the welcome sights and sounds of habitation. In Lime Village lived a man who had been a patient in the hospital in Chiengmai, and who needed more treatment. Recently he had made the long journey down from the hills to join the main road, and then taken the bus some sixty kilometres into the city. When he arrived at the hospital they found his name, looked up his card and, without letting him see a doctor, repeated his medicines and sent him home. He did not need any more of that medicine, in fact he was receiving an over-dose. But he was a tribal person, unable to communicate fluently in Thai, and therefore was assumed to be of meagre intelligence and dealt with accordingly. So he had to take the journey all over again and come down with us, so that the surgeon could see he received the right treatment.

Tribal people are very reluctant to go to hospital when they are sick, because they know they will not be able to communicate. Instead they go to a local 'quack' doctor, usually an unlicensed medicine seller who makes his own diagnosis and sells his wares at an exorbitant price, often leaving the patient feeling worse than he did at the beginning. The bridge to modern medicine takes some crossing for a tribal person.

Medical workers are not the only people to assume that tribal people are somehow mentally backward. Indeed the problem is worldwide. I have seen English people shouting at the tops of their voices to people who cannot speak our language, on the strange premise that increase in volume helps comprehension. I have also known Westerners address highly intelligent and extremely well-educated Chinese people as though they were infants in grade 1 kindergarten, on the mistaken assumption that they could not understand English, when in fact they may have had all their education up to university level in that language. So when government officials in local offices in Thailand treat tribal peoples as lacking in intelligence as well as in education, they have plenty of company. But that does not make it any easier for the tribal person, frustrated at being dismissed as an imbecile. Nor does it help him to make progress in getting things done, or in obtaining justice in a dispute, especially if the other person concerned is a local Thai man or woman. Neither does it help him in his own sense of dignity and personal self-worth. So he does what we all do in such circumstances and withdraws to the security of his own environment, leaving his case to go by default.

Selling produce is no easier. You probably remember those endless sums that some of us would be faced with in our youth: if five men take five hours to dig five holes six feet deep and three feet across, how many people will it take to dig ten holes twice as large? Perhaps those problems used to annoy you as being senseless exercises in futility, or maybe you had one of those brains that seizes upon such meat with a healthy appetite. You can in any case imagine how a tribal person must feel when, having had no education at all, he has to deal with a sum like the following: if corn is 1.83 baht per kilogram and you have 16 sacks to sell which weigh between 83 and 121 kilos, what is a fair price? The tribal person does not know how to divide or how to multiply, so almost inevitably he has to accept the verdict of the middleman and rely on his integrity. Naturally he comes off badly.

The man who came down from the hills and took the bus to hospital had one advantage over some of his contemporaries — he did know where the bus was going. Many tribal people cannot read enough to know what the bus is saying on the front, so they are reluctant to take a bus at all. So once again we come to the basic problem that affects the whole of a tribal person's life: he does not have an education and he cannot read or speak Thai with anything like the fluency required. So the path ahead stretches across the bridge of education, an uncertain bridge indeed for the hill peoples.

It is not only their own needs which compel the tribal people to get involved in Thai society; the government is also determined to integrate them into national life. Most of the tribes were traditionally highly mobile, and many of them have moved across into Thailand under the pressure of political events in neighbouring countries. So they not only have little sense of belonging to the country, but form a reservoir of potentially subversive elements, if the politics of those neighbouring countries spill over into Thailand with them. It is easy to understand the government's concern to ensure that they become loyal citizens committed to the welfare of the country as a whole. The tribal groups, for their part, need leaders who can preserve their cultural heritage and identity, but who can also lead their people over the bridges of change and into a closer relationship with the host community.

With integration come all sorts of other pressures. While the law of Thailand allows complete freedom of religion, not all local officials necessarily appreciate Christianity and sometimes church leaders have been hindered from carrying out their pastoral responsibilities. Part of the problem has been the question of identification, for there is no pastoral uniform to distinguish the church leader from the ordinary farmer. Identification cards issued by the Evangelical Fellowship of Thailand have helped to solve this. But more and more, government welfare agencies and ministries move up into the tribal areas and prove bewildering to people who have never before known this kind of agency. Bangkok is a long way away from North Thailand, light years away in terms of cultural characteristics, so for the tribal person to understand the ways of governments is difficult in the extreme. Many of us have difficulty understanding the ways of our own governments, despite our education, so we can sympathise!

Once again, education is the bridge to change. Facing all the problems outlined above, the Yao church sought to come to grips with them and particularly with the key issue of education. True, the government has been pressing ahead with Thai literacy schools in tribal villages. But these schools do not lead to further educational opportunities, for they are not recognized by the Ministry of Education. So something had to be done to supplement the opportunities available, and to provide the people and the church with the kind of leadership capable of leading them across the bridges of change without too many fatal accidents.

As early as 1974 the Yao church in Nongwaen thought about building a hostel in Maechan to house Yao youngsters studying at high school; but the political events in neighbouring Laos at that time led many people to think of moving away from the area, so the project was shelved. Then in 1976 the newly-formed Association of Yao Churches decided something had to be done. They settled on the idea of a hostel to take up to twenty children of either sex and of all ages, but with preference for those studying at high school.

The next question was, where should the hostel be put? The town of Ngao contains one of the few district high schools offering classes up to university entrance level, and the school has a reputation for high standards. A piece of land or a building came next on the list. In some Asian countries it is frequently difficult to know who actually holds the title to a piece of land, and this problem now cropped up: the missionaries and church leaders discovered several times that the people who had assured them they were the owners of a piece of land were not actually registered as such at the local govern-

32

ment land office. Others assured them that they had the correct title deeds, when in fact the deeds only entitled their holders to use the land, and did not give them ownership. Some people were trying to pull a fast one over the tribal community. Time slipped away and the children were already staying in a Thai house rented for the purpose, but they needed a piece of land on which they could plant vegetables for their own consumption and for sale. In 1979 the right piece of land became available, quite close to the schools in Ngao and at a reasonable price. Fruit trees and vegetables have been planted to provide an income for the hostel, and plans are in hand for a suitable new building to take twenty children plus the houseparents. Eventually there will be room for another twenty children and the people to look after them.

Projects require organization, they do not just happen. The Yao hostel is the project of the Yao church, so as soon as the hostel began to function three of the leading Yao church leaders were set aside to form a hostel committee. They registered the land with the local Land Office, and they act as a standing committee for the oversight of the hostel and as a link between the houseparents and the Yao churches.

Projects also require people to run them, and the failure or success of any operation hangs on the quality of the people available. U Hyang, chairman of the Yao Church Association, had been looking for the right couple for the job for two years. Not very many Yao people could meet the qualifications, and one after another, the people who were approached declined to serve. In any situation of this kind Christians turn to the Lord in prayer, and that is sometimes a dangerous thing to do. As U Hyang prayed more and more about the need, so the Lord laid it on his heart to meet it himself, while at the same time acting as area pastor. Like the disciples when challenged about feeding the five thousand, U Hyang was challenged to give what he had to meet the call.

In 1979 twelve children from six widely scattered villages began living in the hostel, with two boys going to high school, five boys and four girls in various grades at primary school, and one little girl in kindergarten. The district officer, district education officer, and head-masters of both the high school and best primary school have been extremely helpful in their advice. The hostel preserves Yao culture in the daily life and routine, with the children and hostel parents living as a family and each person taking part in the running of the home and the land as he is able. Each child does daily chores, and the older ones spend some time each day weeding and watering the vegetables. The school, on the other hand, immerses them in Thai culture and begins to build the bridge from the other end.

U Hyang and his wife Zeng Gway care too for the spiritual needs of the children. Each evening they gather together for up to an hour of Bible teaching, singing and praying! (There are not quite the same distractions competing for their attention that Western children face. Not all our cultural overlay is progress!) U Hyang's son, one of the high school students, helps with the teaching. On Sunday, some of the Yao who live in the locality join with the family group for a Sunday service.

What part does the missionary play in all this? Very little, as you can see. The missionary can act as a catalyst, helping the church to see what needs to be done and possibly how it can be achieved. No great provisions are needed that are not obtainable locally. Finance for the building of the hostel and the installation of electricity is really the only outside help that is required. The Yao churches provide half of U Hyang's support, and the other half comes from the Home Mission Board of the Bible Training Centre at Phayao. Once launched, the project can easily be self-supporting, but the value to the future of the church and of the Yao people is beyond calculation. The bridge may look rickety, but it does bear your weight and by the grace of God will take you over to the other side.

4 Small is Beautiful

WE live in a success orientated world: you have to 'make it' to be anything, and failure means disgrace. The criteria for measuring success are often artificial too: the bigger the project the greater the success, and the more visible the results in terms of large buildings or big corporations, the more esteem accrues to the person or people involved. Jesus saw things differently. While on earth He conducted a fairly large-scale medical work in terms of people restored to health, but anyone coming along a year after the crucifixion would have found no building to commemorate it, no trust fund to perpetuate it, and indeed nothing very visible to show for it. You would have had to look into the lives of the people, often those of the poor, to find grateful hearts and healed bodies and minds.

I am not seeking to decry the value of hospitals and clinics or to say that large necessarily means ugly, but to draw attention to another kind of work, less visible, more limited in scope in some ways, but where small is definitely beautiful. This chapter concerns a work in Korea which actually rejoiced in an almost fifty per cent reduction in hospital accommodation after three years. The reason for rejoicing is that the incidence of the disease concerned is decreasing and, owing to the discovery of many of those who have suffered from it, fewer new in-patients need beds. (In fact, the hospital was able to be closed altogether by the end of 1981.) To get to the hospital you leave behind the capital city of Seoul and travel to the industrial port of Masan on the South coast. Out of the city and past the scarring ugliness of an iron factory, you climb across a hill to a view of the sea, only then to find the small hospital attached to the Korean Government's programme to deal with children suffering from tuberculosis. The whole project is pocket sized, the staff small, and the man in charge is Dr Peter Pattisson from Britain.

Peter and his wife Audrey first went to Korea in July 1966, convinced God was calling them there. A letter from a respected older Christian, an interview with a senior Christian doctor, and the door to the 70-bed unit in Masan opened. The work also involved supervision of a project for the treatment of spinal tuberculosis. Only four places in the world were tackling such work, and Peter had already had a year of experience at one of them in Africa. Furthermore, he already had links with the Masan area of Korea. God's timing and God's planning are perfect. Peter tells the story in his own words:

*   *   *   *   *

Thirteen years later some things have changed. We started with 70 beds. Now we have 40. We started with 45 staff, now we have 12. Initially we were dominated by the ward work, now we major on out-patients. We began with children, now we take patients of all ages with bone and joint tuberculosis. In those days we drew patients from Masan and the immediate surrounding area only. Now with clinics in three provincial centres we draw patients from east coast to west across the southern half of Korea — a 300 mile span and a population of 15-20 million. Improved transport and a reduction in the total number of patients with bone and joint tuberculosis have allowed this geographical expansion.

Some things have not changed. Our co-operation with the government has been close throughout. It has an overall programme for the treatment of adult lung tuberculosis, but not for bone and joint disease. We use government facilities, live in a government house and complement their programme. On that basis we have enjoyed excellent co-operation. Likewise our concern for the spiritual welfare of staff and patients has not changed. A steady stream of staff and patients who have come to know the Lord testify to the continuing grace of God.

How do we evaluate the work of the last thirteen years?

Firstly, it seems to us that the care of the needy is self-authenticating. With skills and resources available, it would be impossible not to apply them to the help of the sick. 'Wisdom is justified by all her children' (Luke 7.35) would seem to refer back to Luke 7.21, 22 where the Lord cites His healing ministry as authentication of Himself to the imprisoned John the Baptist. Such work is not done primarily in order to prove the truth, still less as bait to lure the unwilling to hear the gospel. However, in retrospect it is powerful testimony to the genuineness of the message, and it is a necessity even in circumstances where it would appear to hinder the gospel (Mark 1.45).

This has been our experience. Often it has troubled us that the demands of our medical work place limits on the time available for direct biblical ministry in the churches. However, looking back, the overall testimony has been far more powerful and we would not have had it otherwise.

Secondly, we rejoice in God's gracious provision over the years. A substantial research grant and the leasing of Korean government premises has meant that we have been able to give free treatment to a group of patients for whom no one else is providing it within their financial resources. Our patients come predominantly from a very poor section of the community and the only payment they make, apart from bus fares to and from the clinic, is the cost of food for in-patients. We have felt this care of the poor within the scope of their resources to be a key part of our work. The Lord's healing ministry was predominantly among the poor and the chronically sick, and we felt ours should be the same. The world says 'God helps those who help themselves', but faith says 'God helps those who help others', and this has been our experience.

Besides our regular basic research grant we have relied on a steady supply of 'bread from heaven' through various sources. Once when drugs were in short supply an order worth over £1,000 placed by another agency was turned over to us *in toto* because that agency had to close its work while the drugs were still in transit. On other occasions the Korean government has supplied drugs, quite unsolicited. On one occasion when a local administrator intent on his own power and profit was doing his best to destroy our work, God removed him and sent a Christian in his place.

At another time we specifically prayed over a period of three months that gifts from overseas sources would be matched by gifts from local sources. During this period income from overseas amounted to £1,819 while that from local sources came to £1,830. We have never turned away anyone whom we felt we could genuinely help within the limits of our facilities, and it has been our privilege to work towards a structure in which the poor feel welcome and not humiliated.

Thirdly, we are deeply grateful for the work of grace that we have seen in the lives of staff and patients. Some years ago one staff member came confessing the things he had lifted from the hospital over a period of some years and asking to have his salary docked in repayment. Asked why he had confessed this, he replied 'When we read the story of the cross, I found that my heart was changed'. His subsequent service in the hospital has demonstrated that change.

While we were on furlough one patient in his late twenties wrote, 'Sir, In a deserted wilderness there was one lost sheep. Everywhere he had wandered looking for his master. At your hospital he has found warmth and kindness and endless patience. That sheep is I, Oo Yong Ee. I am lost in shame to know what to do. I can only cry to the Lord, walk in Christ's path and sing hymns to Him. When you were here always you spoke the joyful words that if only we would seek the Lord He would pour grace upon us. Now I remember these. This weak and sinful Oo Yong Ee is seeking to live carefully by the words of Scripture and although my faith is weak, to seek God's glory.'

More recently another patient, a 14 year old girl, who has had a recurrent septic condition for several years and who is almost totally deaf, wrote 'Immanuel. Loving and merciful Lord. I did not know You, Lord. I used to try believing any religion that said it would make me better. But there was no result, no profit. My heart just got more and more evil. However, since I came to this hospital I have come to know the Father God. At first when I read hymns and the Bible I just read by rote, but little by little my interest was kindled and now I have come to understand. Now by the grace of God and the kindness of the hospital staff, I can see around this beautiful world. Once again, Lord, I say thank you to You. Now Lord, I have come to know what a wonderful and brave Person, You, the Son of God, are. From this time, I too, will learn goodness and follow the Lord. And as I learn many things I will tell them to all my family that they too may know You. Lord, I want to promise before You that I will follow You to the end. I pray all these things in the name of our Lord Jesus Christ. Amen.'

Such testimonies are but samples of a quiet work going on all the time in the lives of patients, which we believe will bear fruit to eternity. The basis of this has been consecutive Bible teaching — the life of Christ and key parts of the New Testament — rather than a series of evangelistic messages and appeals.

Fourthly, we have sought to be a stimulus to local initiative — to evoke the help of local churches, to challenge their unconcern for the refuse of society and to rebuke the exclusion of the poor by much of private medicine, even much of that done in the name of Christ.

Thirty years ago in the Korean War the Korean

Christians responded magnificently to the need of orphans and refugees. In the intervening years the care of the needy has too easily become the province of the foreign organization alone, while the churches devote their energies and resources to enlarging and beautifying their buildings. Secular society has been quicker than Christian leadership to spot the anomaly of this.

By remaining deliberately small, poor and unprestigious we have been able to evoke the co-operation of Christians — church ladies assisting with laundry, groups helping in preparation of food, young people's groups visiting with gifts. In various ways interest and involvement have been stimulated. Said one nominally Christian doctor in town, speaking of our institution, 'You'd need a sense of vocation to work in that place.' It is our hope and aim that by example, challenge and biblical precedent some may be stirred to 'forsake their nets and follow Him' who will lead them into paths of service and blessing.

*   *   *   *   *

Peter and Audrey Pattisson were not members of the OMF when they took up their work in Korea. After a few years it was clear that both they and the Fellowship would benefit from linking together, and he now leads a small team of OMF workers in the country. In the course of those years the Lord has clearly opened a contribution in the Korean church for us, associated mostly with the work of Scripture Union. Korean churches dwarf all but a few Western ones in size yet numbers bring their own problems, one of which is the danger that the average member will be content with church-going as the basis of his spiritual life. We feel therefore that a specific ministry geared to encouraging every Christian to feed upon the Word of God for himself is crucial to spiritual health. The Pattissons have seen the fruit of regular Bible ministry in the hospital and out from it, so that the whole work in Korea is a natural outgrowth of the ministry in which they began.[1]

Sometimes people get frightened by the sheer size of a Fellowship like the OMF, with 900 members from eighteen different home countries scattered across East Asia, from Indonesia in the South to Japan and Korea in the North. Yet each team in its own country of work develops in its own way and functions as a small unit within the larger whole, with the minimum of direction from International Headquarters in Singapore. The Pattissons' ministry illustrates how individual guidance can lead to corporate activity, and also how missionary work today does not have to be the intrusion of a foreign programme from outside. Dr Pattisson has worked all the time in close co-operation with the Korean Government in their medical programme, yet as a full member of the Fellowship. In the same way, others who are members hold university positions, discharging their responsibilities fully and yet openly functioning as members. Today several university Christian Unions and at least one national student movement continue what those people began.

Few would single out Masan Hospital as significant in terms of standards applied in the world today. The work there has shrunk in size. Yet the ripples run across the country, and if you want to see them you must look in the lives of the people, especially of some of the poor. That is where Jesus began. In the light of that, small IS beautiful.

---

[1] *Crisis Unawares* by Peter Pattisson gives many more details about the Church in Korea, OMF's work there and the hospital at Masan, in the light of Matthew's Gospel.

5 To Heal the Sick

JESUS told His disciples very clearly to be involved in the healing of the sick, commissioning them to drive out evil spirits and to cure every kind of disease and sickness. He Himself dealt with the most difficult cases — the lame, the blind, the paralysed, the dead — which are often beyond the reach of medicine even today. With the church's recent rediscovery of the place of healing ministries, no one will be surprised at missions undertaking medical work. But the question 'How should it be done?' is not so easily answered.

Recent medical thinking has moved away from the concept of medical institutions with elaborate buildings and large staff concentrating on the more seriously ill, to that of public health care reaching to the basic needs of the masses, improving general health for the many rather than saving the lives of the few. With governments increasingly taking the provision of hospitals more and more seriously, this process has been accentuated.

Finance is one of the biggest factors to be taken into account. The problem does not lie so much in money from overseas to run programmes — people are ready to give towards that. The real problem arises where the programme is run. Modern medicine is expensive and many drugs have to be imported. Doctors trained in modern Western medical schools often have an acute problem of conscience if they cannot run the full range of tests over every patient; but every test costs money. If the treatment costs too much, then the very people Christians are most concerned to benefit — the poor — get priced out of the market. National churches in developing countries do not abound in money. Therefore if a national programme is envisaged for the future we have to be careful

to keep costs down or to provide a self-supporting programme within the pockets of the lower-paid patients.

The effect on the church presents a second problem.
Institutions require staff and usually there are not
enough Christians to staff them. Therefore a decision
has to be made whether to insist on a Christian profession at a certain level of leadership, or to aim at
medical excellence at the risk of dilution of witness. That
witness is not meant to imply simply aggressive evangelism, but the much wider witness of Christian
standards of nursing and other care, honesty and
integrity. People readily forget that much Western
medical ethics in fact has a Christian base, and where
that does not exist the standard of ethics is different. We
are so used to nurses who give themselves unstintingly
to their work and who have high standards for their profession without necessarily having any personal
Christian faith, that we assume all nurses will have the
same outlook. The concept of nursing as a profession
rather like the civil service, in which certain jobs are not
to be considered because they are below the dignity of a
nurse, may appal us. As for the thought that a nurse
might refuse an injection unless a payment has been
made, the mind boggles. In such an environment a high
standard of dedicated Christian care speaks for itself.

The Christian institution, however, not only brings
the opportunity for positive testimony but also presents
a challenge to Christian living. In areas where
institutions exist, the church may be overshadowed by
the institution and the development of the local church
may become a problem with no easy solution.

Government plans and limitations may give us no
choice in the kind of medicine that can be practised.
More and more, the governments of developing
countries face growing demands from the medical profession within the country to limit the entry of medicals
from elsewhere. Local doctors may prefer to congregate

in the large cities, but sometimes they would rather the country areas lacked adequate coverage than that people were allowed to come in from outside in what looks like competition. Governments have their own plans and priorities, and it is right that they should set them: they have to live with the consequences. Yet this may mean that missions and other overseas contributors to the overall programme cannot do the kind of work that current theory would indicate is best. Do we cease to contribute because we cannot do what we would like to?

With the growth of government projects, the Christian programme may find itself no longer the only practitioner in an area, and then new questions arise. Do we then pack up and go home? What if the hospital or clinic is still providing some aspect of medicine not yet covered elsewhere? Do we seek to hand over the programme to national Christians who will preserve the distinctive contribution of Christian medicine? Where do the staff come from, and how can we be as sure as possible that the Christian testimony will last beyond our immediate successors?

One thing is certain: not everyone will agree on the solution to any of these problems. Another thing which is also certain is that medical work, like all Christian activity, will provoke the attacks of the Enemy. If we want to avoid problems we had better not start. It is comparatively easy to open an evangelistic ministry, and close it again a year later. Indeed, if it grows the chances of leaving it grow too. In medical work, on the other hand, closing down is a big blow to patients and their friends, to staff who have found employment, and to shopkeepers and people involved in transport who suddenly find the people they once served are no longer around. Therefore the problems that arise in medical work cannot easily be disposed of by a stroke of the pen. They demand constant prayerful attention, and Christian integrity prevents oversimplified answers.

People are affected.

When after the exodus from China the OMF was seeking from God a place in which to contribute a medical ministry, Thailand seemed the obvious answer. At that time the rural health services were little developed and most medical work went on in the larger centres of population. Basing their decision on experience gained in China and on the situation in Thailand itself, the leaders of the Fellowship agreed to provide the best kind of service that was available and to be involved in both hospital work and rural clinics for leprosy patients. Three hospitals emerged over the years; the main one out in a country area some 150 kilometres north of Bangkok at Manorom, the second right in the south of the country near the Muslim Malay people, and the third in an even more rural area north east of Manorom. The leprosy work began in a very simple way with clinics in small open shelters. At first there were three such clinics in towns where missionaries lived, but soon the numbers began to grow. By the time there were 2,000 patients there were about twenty centres, and at its height with 3,000 patients there were 45. The number is now diminishing as the government begins to take over some of the clinics. In 1959 a doctor joined the team of six to seven nurses, and now the growth includes not only Thai fellow workers but physiotherapists and occupational therapists. In 1971 the Leprosy Mission seconded a Control Officer to work with the team, and he trains and supervizes a number of Thai paramedical workers engaged in both control and treatment. The programme is integrated with the Government nation-wide programme.

But medical work is not just clinics and hospitals, it is people in need. The story of Mr Toob, one of the first patients, is almost the story of the leprosy ministry. There was no railway or road in his part of the world in those days, only the river. Slowly the little boat travelled, six hours or more from Singburi to Chainat, where he had heard there was a missionary lady who might be able to help him. To his relief the news was true; a missionary did live there and she could treat his disease. That is how the programme was born. Fortunately for Mr Toob, a nurse soon moved to his own town and he did not have to travel. But he began the long journey back to health just as the programme began its long journey to reach out in ever-widening circles to sufferers from this dread disease.

At first the nurse visited Mr Toob at home to give him his supply of pills, and she shared his problems and concerns. Over-protected as a child and teenager, he was shy and withdrawn, helping the family economy by keeping pigs because he could not get other work. When the pigs got sick the missionary shared this problem with him in prayer too, and they recovered. So he had his first encounter with the Living God who answered prayer, and he became a Christian himself.

In 1964 Mr Toob was one of the first patients to have surgery in the newly-opened leprosy wing of Manorom Christian Hospital. The tendon transplants to both feet had excellent results, so that he now walks normally, but surgery to his hand was not so successful. He was appointed Clerk to the wing, and after marrying another leprosy patient looked after the hostel for out-patients. This they did for many years, until their two handsome sons became too big and the flat in the hostel too small, and they had to move out to a larger house. Mr Toob kept on with his work in the leprosy wing, and gave additional help in out-patients. An elder in the local church with a quiet leadership role, like all of us he has had his ups and downs as a Christian. His talents enable him to bring a real contribution to the musical and drama outreach of the church.

Although the number of patients on treatment at any one time remains fairly constant, six to seven thousand have had some sort of contact with the programme over the past 25 years. For many years two out of every three Christians in the Central Thailand plain had come to Christ through their treatment, and even today the majority of members of many churches have had leprosy. Mr Toob is not alone. Others too have had medical and surgical care and been rehabilitated to a full and useful life. Some have needed other help as well, such as physiotherapy, training in new skills, assistance with agricultural occupations like rearing pigs, ducks, or geese, or provision for school clothes and books.

The long-term question is the impact of the programme on the community. Probably the leprosy problem in Central Thailand is less than it was 25 years ago, though this is difficult to prove. Manorom is the only hospital in a large area which has facilities for in-patient care of leprosy complications. It is also the only place where leprosy patients can get treatment for teeth and eye problems. Babies can be born there too, and sometimes adoptions have been successfully arranged.

When we speak of treating the 'whole man' we are not just talking of the physical and spiritual sides of man in contrast with each other. The 'whole man' in a leprosy patient involves numerous areas, for leprosy affects the person and not just the body. There are those who after much time, effort, money, love and prayer just do not overcome their problems. A very few commit suicide; some become beggars; others just drift. Some after months of surgery and physiotherapy, fitted out with good shoes, and seemingly knowing how to care for feet which do not have normal feeling, return after three months with feet as ulcerated as before treatment was started. There are heartbreaks as well as healings.

Mr Dolly was one of the rays of light which make all the effort worthwhile. Neglected and treated like an animal by his family, he not only had leprosy but TB too. He arrived wrapped in a dirty blanket, and for a week he would not unwrap himself. Gradually over a year or more he improved. The TB went and the leprosy came under control, even though he was still badly disfigured and crippled. But, more important, he became a real person. He was able to take part in a drama produced by leprosy patients, in the role of the leading comic! Would his family take him home again? He made the arrangements himself, went back to a new hut, and has made good. He contributes to the family budget by making toys. A regular church member, he is a man with no great gifts, but who can hold up his head with dignity as he takes his place in the local community.

Leprosy is not the only medical affliction in Central Thailand, or in the rest of the country for that matter. To make a contribution in other spheres the Fellowship runs a general medical work based on the three hospitals, Manorom, in the centre, Nongbua, to the north east of Manorom, and Saiburi in the deep south. Manorom provides 80 general beds and 25 leprosy ones. Nongbua has 25 beds, and Saiburi 50. The decision to provide hospital medicine was taken early on, and in spite of much heart searching and negotiating we still feel these institutions have a valid and worthwhile ministry. The sphere of Public Health Care is not open to us in any case, being entirely run by the government.

Come to Manorom on a Tuesday morning and you will find it hard to move in the out-patient department. One side of the waiting area is full of young parents with their bouncing and healthy babies, many yelling at full pitch. The weekly post-natal clinics combine the giving of prophylactic injections with advice on family planning. In the opposite corner, no one looks very sick as women wait their turn for the ante-natal clinic. In the third corner the elderly and frail wait for the eye clinic to start. Good eye treatment is difficult to find away from the big cities and patients come to this one from far and near. In the centre of the waiting space are all the others, with many different conditions and complaints, waiting to see one of the two or three doctors on duty. On the edge of the crowd is a handful of staff, for Tuesday is the day for the staff clinic.

9.30 brings a lull while a Thai staff member or missionary explains what the Gospel is all about, and patients can buy Christian books if they wish to. Special days feature a video tape on the television screens, now installed throughout the hospital. These present not only the Gospel but Health Education in such matters as water, food, and cleanliness. Most of the health education takes place in the ante- and post-natal clinics, and out in the leprosy ones too.

Not that Tuesday is specially busy compared to the other days. Throughout the week specialized clinics deal with surgical and medical problems, skin diseases and leprosy, and paediatrics. Every day a queue of hopeful people waits to be sorted out, diagnosed, treated, sent on to a special clinic, or cured. They come by day and by night, the very sick and the acute emergencies directly to the emergency department and the less urgent cases patiently waiting for the time when the doctor is free. A 24-hour service is something the mission hospital can provide.

The Dental department at Manorom is probably the only one in Thailand outside the main cities to have an oral surgeon. This enables the hospital to provide a special ministry to many who are injured in road traffic accidents, giving them skilled care for facial injuries.

The wards match the busyness of the out-patient department. Every missionary doctor knows the problem of finding a bed for that one extra patient who has come a long way and is too sick to be passed on to another hospital. In the obstetric department about half of the 120 deliveries each month are abnormal. This is because the hospital cannot cope with the large number of mothers who today would prefer to have their babies in a hospital setting. So a restricted number only can be catered for. Inevitably, this means that a large percentage of those admitted have a problem connected with the birth and that in turn means that more care is needed from the staff.

Until quite recently the hospitals were allowed to train nurse aides who could then assist on the wards. In a country with too many people for too few jobs, each year 250 to 300 girls would apply for the 20 or so places available for training. On completing their course many would move on to other jobs, some outside medicine, or in private medical institutions which were glad to employ them because they had a high reputation for hard work and efficiency. Now the hospitals are not allowed to train staff at this level, though a few assistants may be allowed to take a course. Small numbers of other paramedical workers have been trained for X-ray, laboratory, and leprosy work.

The policy of recruiting senior Thai staff has been operative for some time. This has now been accelerated because of the restrictions on training nurse aides locally and the prohibition on new missionary nurses sitting the Thai nurses exam. Taking this and other considerations together, the full indigenization of the medical work at Manorom under its Thai Board is seen as the Lord's direction for this decade.

In each hospital we bear direct as well as indirect testimony to the Gospel of our Lord Jesus Christ. Some will question the soundness of 'taking advantage' of a captive audience of sick people, but a reluctance to do this can be just as much a refusal to treat the whole person, as is preaching to him without providing healing for his sickness. As with all evangelism, the vital point is the attitude in which it is done. If patients are seen as nothing but potential converts, then any response is likely to be artificial and sometimes comes from a desire to please. If, however, patients sense a real concern for them as people, and if that comes across in care for their complaint and a desire to share something precious because they count to us, evangelism does not have to be cold proselytism. Jesus managed to combine healing and teaching with no sense of conflict.

Undoubtedly the biggest test of a medical or any other Christian work's validity lies just here, in the realm of communicating love for the person. Whether it be Public Health Care or hospital ministry, the acid test lies not so much in what is done as in how it is done. Hospitals in Thailand are busy places. In the central plain the temperature rises inexorably from February to June. Then the rains come and cool it down, but bring that other deadly enemy, humidity. Around the hospitals there are no facilities for getting away, and at times to go too far alone may not be safe. Patients flood in daily. Nurse aides have their own personal problems, the Thai staff their own outlook. The missionary is a human being, a sinner saved by grace. Set down in a difficult climate with a new language and culture to learn and with all the ordinary pressures of living in a hospital and little opportunity to escape, she or he seeks to testify by life as well as lip to the power of the Living God. No wonder missionaries are only too conscious of where they fail to communicate that extra in patience, understanding, service, and love that makes all the difference. No wonder they have their own problems in relating to each other day in and day out. No wonder they are the object of enemy attack. Missionary medicine is no soft option, but it is a part of the ministry of the Son of God in today's world.

6 Alcoholics Abounding

SABURO OTA crawled along the beach on all fours. His head was fuddled, his legs no longer responding. The sea washing up on the beach seemed to beckon with a repeated invitation to come and finish it all. There in those waves his restless heart might find peace and his uncontrollable life tranquillity. Yet in the back of his mind something was pulling the other way. His feet seemed to want to go towards the sea, but this something put the brakes on. If only he had been able to rouse his brother from sleep when he had staggered home from his latest drinking expedition, he could have been home asleep by now. Dawn found him still on the beach, but he eventually made it to his brother's house, and they took him once again to the mental hospital. That was the fourth time he had finished up there. His mother had said, 'It's no use. As soon as you get out you start drinking again.' Life for ever in a mental hospital, mixed up with patients suffering from acute mental disorders, seemed to be the only answer.

Saburo Ota was 37 years old and had been raised in a small fishing town on the coast of the Northern Japanese island of Hokkaido. Ten years earlier he had married, but even then he had already been an alcoholic, though he did not realize it at the time. Drink led to divorce, and his wife took one child while he took the other. For the sake of the child he decided to quit drinking. He tried binding a wet towel around his head and saying over and over again that he would not drink. But the power of positive thinking proved futile against the craving, and things went from bad to worse.

Saburo Ota was just one of many Japanese people afflicted with alcoholism. Since the end of World War II the number has increased 400%, with no end in sight, and many mental hospitals are saturated with sufferers from this affliction. Others turn them away, having experienced the 'revolving door syndrome' of people who come in and go out regularly but never make a lasting recovery. Suitable recovery facilities are rare indeed, and under Japanese law alcoholism does not qualify as a disease for receiving social welfare help. So money is available to help the mentally handicapped, but not to provide facilities to assist the helpless drinker. Hokkaido, with 1,800 alcoholics confined in mental hospitals and another 150,000 scattered through society, has a big enough problem on its own, and it is estimated that 6% of the adult population of the country are problem drinkers.

Some groups do exist to help the alcoholic, but less than 1% of those who need such help will go to them, and nearly all are founded on basic humanistic attitudes. Some psychiatrists are sceptical of a religious approach. Others are reluctant to co-operate. Families. acutely conscious of the shame incurred by the alcoholic's behaviour, prefer to keep their relatives in the mental hospital where they can do no harm and where no one need know.

A long way from Hokkaido, on the streets of Chicago, God was preparing a young man for the work to which He was going to call him. Bob Cunningham originally came from a farm background and had a practical bent. For several years he had worked on car engine and body repairs, and he had considerable experience in carpentry, masonry, plumbing and roofing. He had also had a radio-TV repair shop for several years. Since the age of twelve he had considered missionary service and while studying at Bible College had led a prayer band for Africa. Then while at Trinity Evangelical Divinity School just outside Chicago he became involved in work among the alcoholics of Skid Row, and met someone who introduced him to the ministry of the OMF in Asia.

Bob had no idea at the time how those two involvements were to converge in the North of Japan. In the meantime, a young lady from Switzerland named Berti Roth was studying English in England, preparatory to coming to Asia with the OMF. Even from her first term at the Beatenberg Bible School, she had known God wanted her in Japan. Switzerland is the home of a Christian organization called Blue Cross, dedicated to helping alcoholics. Berti arrived in Hokkaido four months before Bob, in December 1971, and Switzerland and America met in language school.

Soon after his arrival in Japan, Bob was introduced to a junk-yard dealer who had usable and repairable items such as refrigerators, colour televisions etc, available very cheaply. Bob's practical nature soon filled an unused room at the language school with a host of miscellany, much of which became very useful to missionaries in an affluent society. The dealer proved to be a recovered alcoholic through whom Bob became aware of the prevalence of drinking problems in Japan and the lack of suitable recovery facilities. While this introduction set Bob on his way to a ministry to alcoholics, the relationship with the dealer led to complications. No one knew too much about the man, except that he wanted to see some facilities established to help people with the problem. His appearance did not commend him — shabby, with clothes obviously picked up from discarded heaps. He also had a bad reputation with the civil authorities, and the standard of his 'Christian' conduct varied with the environment. So while there was already a conviction in Bob's heart that he should be doing something for alcoholics, the beginning was far from auspicious, and eventually the board which had been formed had to ask the dealer to resign.

In August 1973 Bob and Berti returned to Switzerland to get married. Berti's mother had been asked to find a pastor to take the wedding and an evangelical pastor in the next village had agreed to do it. During the honeymoon the pastor came to visit, apologetic for intruding on their time. He explained that the two churches for which he cared might just be interested in Bob and Berti's work among alcoholics. At that time they were still in the middle of language study, not even designated to a specialized ministry like this. The support was forthcoming before the work began, and in fact the regular gifts that came from those churches provided the initial thrust to launch the programme. OMF had not planned to enter a ministry among alcoholics, but God's hand was so clearly shown in the provision of people and support that the Japan leadership agreed to go forward.

How then to begin? The early contact with the junk dealer was not entirely fruitless. People recovering from alcoholism obviously need something to do while they are improving, and before they can manage a full-time job in normal society; the repair of secondhand equipment would provide just the kind of work that was needed. But where could the work be done? At this point, a Christian went for a swim. Not many people swam on that particular beach because lead pollution had ruined it. While on his outing, Mr Sugawara noticed an abandoned pre-fabricated building which had been a shower, and realized it would make an ideal workshop for the infant programme. The city hall kept a file of the owners of such buildings, so Bob and Berti searched him out and offered him all the spare money available right then — only about 10% of the price of such a building when new. The prospect did not look bright. But the man accepted the offer and $540 changed hands. The building was theirs. Four alcoholics travelled on several occasions from a mental hospital to take it to pieces and put it together again. When all was completed there was no money to advertize the opening of the store, but that did not matter for the local press took up the story, and free coverage in a Hokkaido newspaper brought forty phone calls asking them to come and pick up discarded items that they could use. The store opened in May 1974.

Alcoholics began commuting from a mental hospital, but this was not really satisfactory. A half-way house was needed, where patients could live together half way between the confined environment of the hospital and the competitive structure of society. Bob and Berti were looking for a suitable building to rent as living quarters for themselves and for those they were helping, but nothing came up and they had to settle for really cramped conditions. They had one room for themselves and a common kitchen and toilet, while three rooms upstairs provided for the men.

The load was too heavy. A proper home with a Japanese staff was clearly a minimal requirement. By this time a board of directors had come into being, and they agreed that the home would have to be closed until more suitable facilities could be developed. The store continued to operate, and went on while the Cunninghams took a furlough. During their furlough they found the Blue Cross organization in Switzerland really interested in their work, and numerous groups began to give towards the projected centre. Bob was also able to study alcoholism at an American university, so they began their new term of service confidently.

The problem now was to find land on which to build, and that search was to take six months. Bob spent hours driving around the fringes of Sapporo city searching where the environment was good and the land comparatively reasonable in price. Several possibilities arose, but none seemed exactly right. On one occasion, in the depths of the northern winter, Bob borrowed the superintendent's car, only to get caught in a five car pile-up due to the sudden reduction of visibility in a blizzard. Returning home with a damaged borrowed car was no small embarrassment. Berti had her share of anxiety too, waiting for her husband to return through the ice and snow from fruitless forages. Then one Sunday, in the providence of God, Bob 'happened' to visit a new evangelistic centre which had recently affiliated with OMF. One of the key people there, Mr Shibakawa, asked whether Bob had ever thought of that particular area. A short while afterwards, Mr Shibakawa came across a plot of land during one of his morning walks. Located in quiet and natural surroundings, the plot was only ten minutes walk from a major highway and a bus stop. The funds in hand totalled $49,300 and the price was $49,000, one third of the usual for land zoned for building. In June 1977, the purchase was completed.

Land was one thing, a building was quite another. The cost for that could run to double the cost of the land. Nor was money the only problem. Residents of the locality soon discovered that alcoholics might become their near neighbours. Hours of conversation helped to defuse the tension, as did the fact that Bob and Berti were actually going to live in the same building with the men. If they were not afraid to do that, why should the neighbours get scared?

Volunteer workers began to arrive from all over the world in successive small groups, giving themselves and their time. Three came from Switzerland, six from Canada, and others from England, Hong Kong, the USA and Japan itself. One from Switzerland stayed for six months and another for a year. They worked under less than ideal conditions and lived in even less desirable quarters, with the temperature dropping in winter to 20 degrees Celsius and rising in the summer to 35 degrees. Japanese building methods differ from Western ones and this brought frustration too, but slowly the building began to take shape. Meanwhile, Mr Shibakawa had become more involved and eventually became chairman of the board, giving a great deal of time to the work. As the president of a company he was also able to introduce the team to cheaper building materials.

The short term workers not only provided labour, but the very fact of their coming spoke volumes to the neighbours, and earned wide respect. Some of them had already arrived when the land was purchased, but there were not even blueprints for a building and to put in only the foundations required $13,500. Only a few dollars remained in the account. A Christian architect produced a blueprint within a week, and then a Japanese psychiatrist gave enough to complete the foundations. He was not a Christian but respected the work being done.

As the building grew, so did the need for money. Some $10,000 per month were needed for an extended period. The board had to make a decision on principles, and although not tied to OMF policy, they agreed to accept the principles on which the Fellowship has functioned for over a hundred years. They would not go into debt, nor appeal for money. At that time someone in Canada offered to come to help with the carpentry. But supposing he came and there was no money for wood? Discussion rolled to and fro, but eventually it was agreed to go ahead and have the help come, believing that God would supply the materials to match the skills. Only once in the forthcoming months did they have sufficient funds to be able to see their way ahead. On one occasion, $10,000 was needed on a certain day and only $3,000 had come in. On the morning when payment was due the postman had no letters for them. Bob called the Sapporo OMF office to see if anything had come there. Nothing. Finally, half way through the afternoon, the bank called to tell them that a gift over and above what was needed had been deposited in their account.

Meanwhile, volunteer workers went on erecting the major part of the building, including the foundations, much of the walls and ceilings, and the painting. Not only was the work being done, but for less than half price! Volunteers too received their share of blessing.

One young man from Switzerland had met the Cunninghams during their first furlough, when he was nineteen years old and had just completed his apprenticeship as a mason. He offered his help and was one of the first to come, even before the money for the foundations was available. While out in Japan he was baptized, and stayed long enough to see the foundations completed. At the same time, another young couple came across from the States for several weeks. Now the Swiss young man lives with the young couple's parents in America while he attends the same Bible School that they did. Through the Urbana Conference he has dedicated his own life to missionary service, and looks forward to possibly returning to Japan.

Not all the gifts came from overseas — the Lord also moved Japanese Christians to give. One day a registered letter, from a person the Cunninghams had never met, brought a postal draft for $5,000. Someone else not only gave a considerable sum but introduced them to his brother who immediately produced a cheque for $5,000. Some of the gifts were small, but all were valued as the miracle went on.

Eventually in November 1978, around two hundred people arrived at the new building for the dedication. But the problems were not over. Some psychiatrists and hospital directors did not want to co-operate. A few had a reputation for not discharging patients, and some families did not want to run the risk of their relatives leaving the home and embarrassing them. In the end, three men entered. The moods of one rose and fell like a barometer. The second seemed interested in religion, until he found it impossible to accept his own sinfulness. The third had already been in hospital for seven years and easily became sick. Dissatisfied and grumbling, all three made little progress and in January 1979 they all walked out. Back to square one. Although these men have managed to keep free from drink, they were not the kind of human foundation on which to build a work.

Soon a man from south of Tokyo arrived, recommended by some Swedish missionaries. On his way up to Hokkaido he was still drinking, but he has stayed sober since. Then Mr Kamakura who had been commuting to the store came to live with Bob and Berti. These two men began to read their Bibles and to pray. Then others joined the group from unexpected places, some from mental hospitals and others straight from the outside community. The day began with a devotional meeting, with a more formal kind of Bible study once a week. A sense of belonging was beginning to grow.

Since then numbers have steadily increased, and now volunteer psychiatrists, case workers and doctors co-operate in conducting group meetings and lectures. Twenty hours a week go on work therapy, and on Saturdays, a group of hospital recreational directors come to supervise group games. The programme aims at restoring men to society within four to twelve months, even though relatives wish them to stay longer.

Pastor Utsonomiya who once suffered from alcoholism himself, now helps in the running of the home. A housewife helps to keep track of the finances. Some of the residents themselves show good potential for future staff help, and while in the home assist in cleaning, cooking, and household duties. In October 1979, due to sagging sales and increased overheads, the secondhand store had to be closed. However, a new work therapy opened up with a furniture company being prepared to sub-let the work of making mats to support the mattresses of bunk beds. In addition, a sizeable farm that can be rented reasonably has become available nearby. A semi-retired farmer has offered to do all the work requiring farm machinery, and so another opening for work therapy and support has been provided. Eventually the home will accommodate thirty men and will need another full-time helper. Only recently the government authorities informed the board that men entering the home qualify for welfare money. According to the Christian psychiatrist on the governing body this is the first time in the history of Japan that a home has been recognized in this way.

What happened to Mr Saburo Ota?

One day Mr Ota's brother was watching television and saw that some missionaries had just opened a home for alcoholics. He went round to his brother with the news. 'Why don't you give it a try?' he asked. So on February 10th, 1979 Saburo Ota arrived at the home. In his desperate need he responded to the Gospel and gave his heart to Christ. In July, after attending the OMF-affiliated Kawazoe church in Sapporo city for the intervening months, he was baptized. On August 10th, having completed the six months rehabilitation programme, he offered to work for the home if there was something to do. After passing his driving test he became the driver of the home's 26-passenger bus. He now supervises all of the work therapy in the home, and is quick to sense the pulse of the men so that problems which might otherwise have grown to unmanageable proportions can be contained at the start. Recently the phone rang and his wife was on the line, offering to send him a picture of the two children, both of whom by that time were living with her. He does not know whether she has remarried or not. If not, there is still hope in the providence of God for a reunion and a remarriage, the joining again of a broken family. Even as a Christian, he still at times has a great temptation to drink, but now he can endure these periods and so far has not once succumbed. Part-time Bible training at the Hokkaido Bible Institute is his next step forward in a life renewed by the Gospel in social action.

Mr Naniwa entered the home four days before Mr Ota. He worked in construction and frequently had to be out of town where, lonely away from home, he would drink to help himself get to sleep. But drink took over, and eventually a distracted wife, who had been to the Salvation Army Sunday School in Sapporo in her early days, brought him to the home with the alternatives of recovery or divorce. He and Mr Ota became friends, and he too responded to the claims of Christ and was baptized. After six months in the home he was able to return to his wife and child, and now leads his family to church each Sunday. His former employer has asked him to return to the company, with a guarantee of no Sunday work and fewer out of town assignments. Although a period of five years is none too short to see whether a person has fully recovered, the men have been showing increasing response, and more than a dozen of them have found a new source of power and comfort in Jesus Christ.

Does modern, sophisticated, affluent Japan need social work? One would hardly think so. And yet here was a need not being met, and a man and his wife called to meet it. They have never wavered from their primary calling as missionaries. The programme has not meant large sums in foreign aid, and apart from the short-term volunteer workers only one couple has been involved. Perhaps it does only touch the fringe of a need, but signs are not wanting that this ministry could be the start of something that could spread. The missionary's role in that case will have been simply that of a catalyst. We believe in that kind of social action.

7   From Miseries to Ministries

'BEFORE you brought the Gospel to these people we could do what we liked, but now they are no longer afraid of us.' 'Before you came, nobody cared about us. We were treated like animals.' These are two actual comments made from opposite sides of the fence in Mindoro island in the Philippines. One remark came from a lowland lawyer frustrated at having to sort out the claim of some Mangyan tribespeople to forest land they had occupied for many years, the other from a tribesperson walking along the trail. How you view social action depends upon your viewpoint.

The Mangyan consist of six tribes of hill people who inhabit the island of Mindoro. Used to the jungle and the forest, and accustomed to a very simple way of life, they felt like a sledge hammer the impact of land hungry lowlanders moving into their island territories. OMF began work among the Mangyan back in 1951 and by the late seventies there were forty organized churches, a joint Bible school, and a Mangyan Tribal Church Association uniting the churches together. Very soon after starting witness among them, the missionaries came to realize that social issues were far from peripheral to their ministry.

Land grabbing was one of the first problems to force itself upon them. Lowlanders would sometimes come carrying pieces of paper which they represented as deeds to the land the tribesmen had cultivated all their lives. Not being able to read or understand the implications, and fearful of aggressive outsiders, the Mangyan would move off higher up the mountain. Other intruders would offer the unwary tribesman a tiny pittance for his land and, ignorant of the value of money, the family would move off. Caroline Stickley has told me how one day a tribesman picked up some little stones and a bit of dirt, and looking mournfully at the missionaries he said, 'Everybody is trying to take our land away from us, telling us that we should go to live further into the interior. But the land is like this.' Tossing the stones and dirt into the air he went on, 'It is very stony in the interior, and we'll die of starvation because the land won't produce anything.'

Nor did the problem stop with deceit. Balud and Win-ay lived in a settlement visited regularly by missionaries. Across the river from the village, lowland people held land under a lease that allowed them to pasture cows on it. At the same time, they were planting crops on the Mangyan land in order to be able to claim it as theirs in the future. A father and his son-in-law held the lease and the father had often threatened to kill the Mangyan. One night the missionaries were holding literacy classes for the community, and Balud and Win-ay were the only couple not to attend. They lived out of sight and hearing of the house where the classes were being held. At dawn the next day Win-ay appeared at the missionary's house with a wound in the back of her head. During the night, while they and their eight-year-old son were asleep, one of the lowlanders had broken into the house, bound Balud and cruelly beaten him about the head. As Win-ay tried to escape through another door, she too was grabbed, her hands were tied behind her back, and she was hit in the back of the head. When she later regained consciousness, her son untied her hands and they both hid in the bushes outside until daylight. When she found her husband he was dead.

Other injustices soon became apparent. A missionary and a tribesman stood staring at the empty huts and silent shacks of a deserted hamlet. During their gruelling two-hour climb they had been looking forward to the joyful welcome and to the more-than-compensating days of Bible training for which they had come. But no one was around. They waited in one of the houses and after a long time the headman and church leader appeared with the sad explanation. It was nearly harvest time, and the rice *had* looked like doing well, when for the third year in a row the owner of a nearby cattle ranch had opened his fence and let his fifty cows loose on the crops. By the morning little remained for a year's work, and the Mangyan were out in the forest, foraging and digging for anything eatable to keep their families alive.

Typhoons frequently hit Mindoro, and in 1978 one community of Mangyan suffered particularly badly. Three successive powerful typhoons did a thorough job, and the last one hit during the harvest. In these circumstances, a 'kind friend' soon offered a loan of seed and time to repay. But at next harvest time he would be back again, claiming his repayment plus half of the new harvest. In addition, the Mangyan, not realizing what was happening, would have carried the harvest down to the plain without any charge whatsoever. What little was left might well be bought by a trader who knew that the price was low during the harvest season, but it would soon go up again when the Mangyan had run out of rice.

In *Broken Snare,* Caroline Stickley mentions an occasion when a group were sitting outside the house. A lowland man came by, dragging with him lengths of rattan which the tribesmen with great effort and sweat had hacked down in the forest. 'I need this,' was all he said. The tribesman's wife yelled after him, 'Hey, you can't take that — it's ours. That's stealing.' He just kept on walking. They had what he needed, so he took it. 'It's very difficult,' said the tribesman, 'but it's always like that. They take anything of ours they want, and they never pay us for it, even though they've got more money than we'll ever have.'

A missionary happened to be in a shop when a proud young tribesman was deciding which of the many bush-knives on display he wanted to buy. Digging in his bag, he found his beautiful little self-made purse, withdrew a rather large bill and handed it over to the lady behind the counter. She was already asking a fabulous price for the tool, but he did not know that. Nor did he have any means of knowing how much change he should receive. Previously he would have paid a piglet or two, or some rice at harvest time. That particular young man was fortunate that there was someone in the shop at the time to see he had a fair deal, but that does not often happen.

Not only are the people vulnerable to injustice, but they are also open to severe medical problems. Two brothers wanted to get some honey out of a hive in a tree. They built some makeshift scaffolding, lit a fire at the base of the tree to keep the bees away and began to climb. The scaffolding collapsed and both the men landed in the fire. Both were badly burned, but one was much worse than the other. The less injured one made his way down to the Mangyan Bible School, arriving at about 5 pm with the news that his brother was following, carried in a makeshift sling swinging from the shoulders of two relatives. They arrived well after dark with the man in a state of shock. His injuries were too serious to be dealt with on the spot, so after the staff had done what they could for him the sad procession had to walk further down the hill and out to the road. They could not hurry because of the pain to the sufferer and they did not reach the road till around midnight, only to find no sign of the 'Jeepney' (a cross between a taxi and a mini-bus) which the brother had ordered to take them to Calapan Hospital. The driver had presumably given up on them and gone home. After more delays while they raised another driver from sleep and convinced him that the journey had to be made at once, they were on their way again. Twelve hours after the accident, at 2 am he finally reached the hospital. Within a few days he was dead.

Medical emergencies can happen in the most advanced societies. What most people do not face, however, is the kind of experiences faced by Arding, a little grey-haired grannie who lives three hours walk upriver from the nearest road. She does not know how old she is, but somewhere between sixty and seventy would be about right. She has lived all her life in the same village and she and her husband Lino were married when she was only nine. Of her eight children, only two are still alive. When the eldest child was three an epidemic of gastro-enteritis hit the village, and he and ten others died from dehydration due to diarrhoea. The third child died from measles that led to pneumonia, and the fourth and fifth both died of malaria. The seventh was married when she was ten and within a year was dead from tuberculosis. Arding had real problems when the eighth child was coming. That year a typhoon had destroyed the crops and they were forced to live on what they could find, which was usually sweet potatoes. That left her very anaemic, so the baby was born prematurely and quickly succumbed. Arding only just survived the resulting haemorrhage herself.

For most of this period of their history, Arding and Lino had no resort but to spirits and charms, until eventually the Gospel reached their community. Their story echoes the common lot of so many of the hill people, in terms of susceptibility to disease and lack of knowledge, how to prevent it and how to cope with it when it hits.

The missionaries who brought the Gospel to these people could not ignore their general need. Without land to cultivate, they would soon be starved out of existence. In the face of injustice, they had no defence. When disease threatened they had no knowledge or facilities to cope with it. The Gospel was changing the lives of the people, but not the cruel pressures that threatened to extinguish them from the face of the earth.

Bob and Joy Hanselman were compelled to become involved when Balud was murdered and Win-ay appeared on their doorstep in the morning. The Mangyan would simply have buried the body and lived from then on in fear of further violence, laying the blame on their own people. So Bob carried the corpse down to the river, and he and Joy joined the people in keeping animals away until the next day when the town doctor performed an autopsy. The Mangyan then reported the case to the authorities and from then on the only role the missionaries played was that of interpreter in the court proceedings. The case took a very long while to come to a conclusion and it was only after 36 hearings that the three accused were eventually sentenced, first of all to death, which was later commuted to life imprisonment.

Often the missionaries were faced with situations in which they just did not know what to do or how to advise the people. In those early days the church was only just emerging and the demands on time and energy involved in pioneer ministry left little opportunity for thinking through a concerted plan to tackle other problems. Then gradually a few interested Christian professionals and students from Manila began to visit Mindoro occasionally with the desire to help in any way they could. Not very much was in fact done, but during the five years or so that this phase continued, several key people became exposed to the Mangyan scene and needs. One Christian lawyer in particular became very involved, and was instrumental in forming the Philippines Christian Lawyers' Fellowship during the second half of the 1960s. At about the same time the Inter Varsity Christian Fellowship in the Philippines began to send occasional teams of medical personnel to help the Mangyan communities.

Sheer necessity called for more and more involvement from the missionaries during this period, and it was at this time too that Andreas and Ruth Fahrni arrived, specifically to help with the agricultural needs of the community, and later to be involved in general planning and supervision. Between 1965 and 1973 the main help was provided by the Christian Lawyers' Fellowship, with Attorney Bongco himself spending a considerable amount of time on the job in Mindoro. Other local lawyers became interested in helping to solve land disputes, and so the social action side of the work developed slowly into something more formal.

Rather than allow the social ministry to grow haphazardly, everyone involved realized that a concerted effort had to be made to provide regular assistance. The key was felt to be, rather than continually adding to the professionals visiting from Manila, to develop a self help programme which would eventually enable the Mangyan themselves to stand on their own feet and care for most of their own basic needs. At about the same time, OMF became aware of the German Agency in Bonn which had helped finance similar programmes in other parts of the Philippines, and which had attached to it experienced people who would give wise advice on pitfalls to be avoided.

It is not necessary to go into the whole history of this programme as it evolved through several years. Suffice to say that the early days were full of difficulties, and at one point the whole programme had to be completely re-organized. We had not been this way before. Eventually, however, the programme became what it is today, the Mangyan Development Programme operated by the Mangyan Tribal Church Association themselves. It is a four-year integrated self-help project of community development, through land security and legal assistance, agricultural development, trading centres, literacy and adult education, and public health. The land security and legal assistance aim to deal with some of the worst of the injustices, and the trading centres to protect the people from exploitation. Literacy and adult education will enable the people to do their own negotiating on equal terms, and agricultural and medical programmes seek to improve basic skills and knowledge. The project aims to have ten centres operating at the end of the period, without the need for outside help in terms either of experts or money.

To run this programme the Tribal Church Association appointed a Project Council consisting of two of their own members, one suitably qualified local person, and one OMF missionary, all resident in Mindoro itself. Under them was the executive officer of the programme and under him the heads of the individual programmes eg, medical, agricultural. Instructors functioned under the heads of the programmes to help clarify areas of need, teach their own speciality to the Mangyan, supervise the work of trainees, teach the whole community the value of the programme, and find suitable ways of working that could be easily copied and put into practice by the people themselves. This structure will change as the programme develops.

The land security programme helps the Mangyan to realize that they have to lodge a claim with the appropriate government department and assist them to gain security for the use of such land. The agricultural programme aims to correct such major problems of the community as malnutrition and poverty. Food supplements for a more balanced diet can be taught by the introduction of 'backyard gardening'. Mindoro has two distinct climatic regions, so these differences have to be allowed for. When more cash crops are grown, then the trading centres can provide both marketing outlets and the seed and other agricultural supplies needed for successful development. The adult education programme aims first of all to help the people on to literacy, and then to enable them to relate to the majority community outside and to take their full part in normal

71

Philippine society.

The medical programme is primarily one of public health, placing emphasis on preventive as well as curative medicine and including such subjects as sanitation, nutrition, health education, home medicines and dentistry. Sixty Mangyan 'barefoot doctors' have been trained and work under a medical supervisor, while the whole scheme will cooperate closely with the Government health programme and with nearby hospitals for dealing with emergencies. Any Mangyan community can decide to take part in this programme, whether they are Christian or not, but it does have to be restricted to the six tribes for obvious reasons. The medical programme is limited by what can be done in the way of self-help and community development, for it has to stand eventually on its own feet. The aim is to avoid establishing an 'elite' of people in the know, but rather to encourage the whole community to be involved in dealing with what is within their power to tackle. Such matters as pneumonia and diarrhoea can be dealt with in this way, but when problems like tuberculosis arise which are outside their power to cope with, then the programme aims to train them to know how and where to get the right kind of help.

The emergence of an integrated programme of development for tribal communities takes us a long way from the early days, when to gain the confidence of a group of tribespeople long enough for them to listen to what the missionary had to say was a major achievement. Yet ministry to these people could not stop with the preaching of the Gospel and still remain credible. In some ways they were specially suited for the emergence of a self-help development programme. Because they are self contained, clear limits were set to the programme. Not having to restrict it to any one part of the community, such as to believers, eliminated the problem of people believing in order to gain material help. Because they are at a very early stage of social development, a little help goes a very long way. Because they are a distinct and minority community, help to them does not have the political repercussions it could have if given to lowland communities. Perhaps the most encouraging aspect of the whole matter is that, we trust, eventually the Mangyan themselves will be running the whole programme without outside help or outside money, and they themselves will see their miseries being met by ministries that they themselves are staffing.

The missionaries have never lost sight of the aim of preaching the Gospel, with which it all began. In fact the Mangyan Church has not lost sight of that aim either. Concrete evidence of this lies not only in their continuing outreach to their own communities deep in the interior of Mindoro island itself. They have also sent their own missionaries across the sea to neighbouring Luzon island, to bring the same Gospel to unreached Negrito people in the Bicol district of that, to them, distant shore.

8 Broken Pieces

THE wind blows and the curtain billows. The precious porcelain topples for a moment on its base, then dives to the floor and shatters. All that is left is broken pieces, shattered reminders of something that once was a coherent whole to be looked on with pleasure.

Invasion strikes. Subversion succeeds. The winds of change whistle through a country from one end to the other. The people are struck, and many of them fall or flee to join the shattered remnants of what was once a coherent nation in the mass of broken pieces that make up the refugee communities of our divided world. We have seen it again and again in our 'progressive world', and not least in the nations of the Indo-China peninsula, Vietnam, Laos and Cambodia. To what purpose is this waste?

Those words take me back to another scene as Jesus dined with Simon the Leper. A woman came into the company carrying a precious jar and broke the vessel, this time deliberately, and poured the contents on the head of Jesus. But now the broken pieces had a meaning, one much deeper than even the woman herself could see. Still there was at least one bold enough to voice the question, 'Why this waste?' Surely the thing to do at a time like that was to sell such expensive perfume and give the money to the poor. After all, it was worth a year's wages! Jesus Himself, the friend of the poor and outcast, the one who told the rich that it was easier to pass through the eye of a needle than to enter the kingdom of heaven, this same Jesus was the One who came to the woman's defence. She had performed a necessary function, the significance of which was totally lost on her contemporaries.

When missions face the dilemma of the broken pieces

of life among refugee peoples, they face a similar problem of priorities. Clearly at the start physical needs prevail. When a person has crawled through cruel jungles and minefields, past hideous booby traps and watchful patrols of the implacable rulers of his own land, to reach the safety of a refugee camp in Thailand, he needs physical help. Usually clad in filthy rags, and suffering from a mixture of malaria, malnutrition, beri-beri, dysentery, skin diseases, parasites and wounds, he needs washing, clothing and medical attention first. Don Cormack, who since 1975 has worked among these people, tells how refugees always remember that first touch of human care which they have met for a very long time. As they slowly return to life and to some semblance of normality they may forget many things, but they never forget that first encounter.

Ministry of this kind is clearly recognized by a wide variety of organizations, many of which would not claim any allegiance to Jesus Christ, and might even specifically reject such allegiance. Caring and compassion are not a monopoly of the Christian community. The United Nations High Commission for Refugees plays a large part in refugee relief, as does the International Red Cross which has coordinated all the medical work among Indo-Chinese refugees in Thailand. At the end of 1979 at least sixty doctors and over one hundred nurses from various agencies were available for medical ministry there, and in fact at that time saturation point had been reached for personnel of all kinds. Among Christian agencies were World Vision, CAMA Services of the Christian and Missionary Alliance, Southern Baptists, TEAR Fund, South East Asian Outreach and Christian Outreach.

In this context, any decision about priorities needs determination, prayer, and wisdom. In one sense the need itself in all its vastness cries out to be met. In another sense people can be rushing around being busy doing good, treading on each other's toes in the process of meeting similar needs. However for missionaries with a knowledge of the language and the people coming out of both Cambodia and Laos, the spiritual need was a clear priority. To heal the hurts of the body is vital to survival. To clothe the people who have dragged themselves across the border in their worn and torn rags stands out equally as a pressing need, but can be done comparatively quickly. The hurts of the heart are in another category altogether.

Many of the refugees from Cambodia have not only lost their homes and land, but their families and friends and their hope of reunion and a settled future. They arrive in a country already facing severe economic pressure, and understandably the local people look askance at the provision made for these latecomers, when they themselves have been struggling for years to eke out a living from reluctant soil. The local government authorities live on the horns of the dilemma — sheer humanity requires that help be given, and yet the more that is given the more their own people become unhappy. So the refugee does not feel his neighbours want him. He does not know where he is to go to. Back home is hopeless. Third countries are not only selective as to who they take, but mean he must face a whole new set of problems in the shape of climate, culture, joblessness and language. If from an aristocratic background he may be shocked and disappointed by the treatment he receives. If he stays where he is he is frustrated too. Many of the Hmong who have moved out of Laos and are now confined to refugee camps were used to roaming the forests or working the fields, often miles from home; the confinement is intolerable. Bereavement in itself is a great emotional shock to the system, as many of us know, but to be bereaved of country, family, familiarity, future, health and wealth, all in one stroke, is impossible even to imagine.

In such a situation the spiritual needs of the people must receive attention, and here the missionary comes into his own. Not that others always understand. Some organizations have sought to prevent Christian ministry among refugees, complaining that to 'proselytize' within the camps is to take advantage of people in need. They see the Gospel as a form of propaganda, another ideology, an attempt to bring people's viewpoint into accord with our own. Often this concept of the Gospel is accompanied by a somewhat idealistic notion of the character of other religions and their central place in the culture of the people, and is met with in those responsible for resettlement in third countries as well as in the camps. However, such rejection of specifically Christian witness cannot lessen the missionary's commitment to the proclamation not of an ideology but of the love of the living God and the reality of the power of Jesus Christ to raise from the dust those whose lives have been demolished. If the Gospel is true it corresponds with reality and is true for all.

In the Cambodian camps, the desire of the missionary to share the Gospel has been matched by the eagerness with which many have grasped at literature and at an opportunity to know what the Gospel is all about. Some had heard something of it in earlier and happier days. Others have listened to messages from the Far East Broadcasting Company, sometimes on hidden radios during the dark days of the Khmer Rouge* regime. Just as in Pnom Penh before the fall of the city, so in the camps, people began immediately to turn to the Lord. Though without pastors, evangelists or leaders, these new believers formed strong churches in the camps. Don Cormack describes the process as being rather like building a church in a railway station, with a constant flow of people in from Cambodia and out to third

* The Chinese-backed Communists under Pol Pot, who ruled Cambodia from April 1975 to January 1979.

countries. No sooner were one set of leaders trained than they disappeared over the horizon and the process of training had to be done all over again.

One major area in which missionaries can contribute is literature. The Khmer Rouge ruthlessly exterminated the educated class of Cambodian society, but when compelled to leave the country the missionaries had picked up a copy of every Christian book they could find, and these have been reprinted in Thailand. So almost the only Cambodian literature in the refugee camps is Christian, and people eager for something to read grasp at what is available; many as a result find themselves drawn towards Jesus Christ. Very few of the refugee workers in the camps can speak any Cambodian and work mainly through interpretation. So when the missionary comes with some knowledge of their language, and books and pamphlets as well, he receives a warm welcome.

Yet some of the most significant movements in the camps have arisen among the believers themselves, some of whom are very young in the faith and often young in years too. When Pastor Som decided in October 1979 that his church in N.W. Cambodia had to move out to the Thai border to seek food, he led some 25 believers out with him. Once in a safe place, they testified boldly of the Lord's keeping over the years of terror, without a trace of bitterness for the sufferings they had endured. People gathered around them as the pastor clutched his tattered Bible, so worn down that it began in Genesis 8 and finished in Revelation 11. Later on, the Thai government allowed thousands of these Cambodians to cross the border to a holding centre at Khao I Dang. By Christmas that year several thousand gathered in the open to worship the Lord, led by Pastor Som and other former elders and Bible School graduates who had found their way into the camp. The church mushroomed; fifty house churches soon emerged and became centres for Bible teaching and prayer meetings. In the main church, whose erection was permitted by the UN High Commission for Refugees, people met to pray all night for their stricken country. Don Cormack himself was involved in teaching basic Christian truths to several hundred potential leaders each week, and speaks of the church standing out like a light set on a hill, against the louring background of dark despair, self-centredness and uncertainty.

Another of the missionary workers, Alice Compain, is also an accomplished musician who has taught herself to play Cambodian instruments as well as her own violin. As she plays, she draws her bow across strings in tension, tightly held at one end and tightly wound at the other. It is the tension which makes the music pleasurable — a slack string utters only a groan. And so Alice herself lives under the constant tension of meeting both the physical needs of refugees in the transit camp in Bangkok — warm clothing for new countries — and the spiritual needs of those same people, as they move out of all that is familiar and into the materialistic wilderness of Western society. Nor does the ministry stop when they have flown out of Thailand. Many refugees write back from their new homes, sharing their problems and heartaches or enquiring about family members from whom they have not heard. Constantly the tension is there: on what should I spend my time today? The answer lies neither in the realm of the physical, nor in the realm of the spiritual. In fact, it is the barrier between the sacred and the secular which lies in broken pieces around the refugee ministry. Human lives cannot be categorized when all their needs cry out for help, and not to meet any of those needs is to fail in our responsibility. Yet many of those engaged in ministry to refugees have no touch with the spiritual dimension, which places all the more responsibility upon those who do.

To tell the story of the refugee camps is not the

purpose of this book. That has been and is being done elsewhere. The point I want to make is that involvement with a people in mission has no stopping place. Artificial barriers between the sacred and the secular, the physical and the spiritual have to disappear. And once involvement has begun it has to go on. The only way to stop with any integrity is not to start at all. We had no idea that sending missionaries to Laos and Cambodia would lead to ministry of different kinds in camps up and down Thailand from the North to the South East, and in at least twelve people being involved in a variety of ways from knitting to Bible teaching, cassette tapes to name tapes. Nor does this tally take account of those whose ministry has been in France or Britain or America. Their kind of work involves long hours on the road to visit a group here or a group there, to encourage them in the midst of a difficult cultural readjustment, perhaps local resentment in the hard-pressed competition for jobs, or the sapping disease of materialism bringing on atrophy of the soul. Nor does it take account of national Christians and the host of part-time helpers who have been drawn in.

Putting broken lives together requires the strength of an ox, the flight path of an eagle, the courage of a lion, and the thoughts of a human mind. Like the creatures who surround the throne in Ezekiel or Revelation, the servants of the Lord must be prepared to face all ways at once and maintain their direction and their co-operation with each other. The team may be quite small in number, and its financial expenditure may not be counted in millions, but hope sown in the hearts of believers goes a long way and multiplies like yeast.

In a year or two the camps may well all be gone from Thailand. Those who have not succeeded in getting to third countries or who did not want to do so could be back home, or at least back in their own country. Already plans are in hand to close most of the camps in 1982.

80

Whichever way people go, they need some sort of glue to put the broken pieces of shattered lives and families together again. Many of the pieces are missing and some will never be found. Some lives are shattered beyond recall. Without some binding substance to hold them together, the future looks bleak. But the Gospel of Jesus Christ is a Gospel of love, and love is the fastest-setting glue in the history of personal relations! When we can see what it does in the darkest of situations, we cannot stop our ministry to refugees at the physical or even emotional level. Not only Christianity but true humanity compels us to go on to introduce people to the One who, as Himself One in Three, knows all about joining people and lives together.

9 Bread for the World

WHEN Jesus reminded the devil that Man does not live by bread alone, He was pointing beyond the material needs of man to those that lie deeper. But He was not saying that man does not need food. Obtaining the basic necessities of life is the major concern of multitudes in the world today, and Jesus did teach us to pray, 'Give us this day our daily bread'. Therefore in presenting the Gospel of Jesus Christ as that which meets the deepest needs of the human heart, missionaries cannot ignore the clamouring need for elementary provision. Many government scientists and agriculturalists give their full attention to the problem, with resources in finance and expertise far beyond that of missions. Yet even so the individual missionary may be able to bring that added emphasis which keeps a programme from becoming concerned with bread alone. In fact, more often than not bread (or rice) is only one of the problems. Time and time again phenomenal growth in food production has been outstripped by population growth, leaving some countries worse off than they were before. Control of pests may also be more urgent than producing more in the fields for the pests to eat in the granaries.

The Christian agriculturalist has an obvious opportunity for service in this context. Sometimes the only question to be decided is whether he or she should link up with some existing government programme, or seek ministry through a mission. The two alternatives are not necesssarily exclusive. The OMF has always welcomed Christians who wish to share in full membership, but who also share our vision of a world for Christ and see a place for their skills within that context. The agricultural or scientific specialist does not necessarily have to go out without a close link with a mission, or with only the somewhat tenuous link of a special category of membership. There are some real advantages in full membership of a mission.

One of these advantages is that the specialist can then be prepared through orientation and language programmes for adjustment to and immersion in the culture of the host country. When English is not the main language of the country, the specialist without language training may find himself or herself unable to communicate at anything but a superficial level with people outside the work context, and this can be very frustrating indeed. The deeper contact with national fellow workers which language and orientation provides can make a difference in every realm, including effectiveness in the job to be done.

A second advantage lies in the pastoral care that a mission should be providing for its members. Not every Christian transferred suddenly to a new culture and climate can function well on his own. There may not be a local church or fellowship in sight, and even if there is its members may not understand the particular stresses and strains being faced by the foreign worker. For them everything is normal, so why should there be a problem?

A third advantage may be that if the mission is really in touch with the churches of the land and with the openings available to expatriate personnel, then it may be able to link the specialist with the most useful opportunity available. This may not be the most prestigious opening around, but it may be the one with a wide influence for good, or the biggest impact on the community.

Some people may feel that being a member of a mission will create the wrong image in the eyes of the authorities. That is not necessarily so. The important point is to be honest about the attitude the person adopts. So long as the specialist is capable of doing the job well and is not going to use his position simply as a springboard for evangelism to the detriment of the work, the authorities may in fact prefer to have a person with convictions rather than someone without strong standards, or with the wrong kind. In Asia, religion is not the banned subject of conversation that it is in the West. In one country a strong proponent of another religion was informed that a new member of his staff was in fact an OMF member and would therefore have strong convictions. He was delighted. 'This country needs that kind of person with deep religious ideals,' was his response.

John and Ruth Chambers are both well qualified, John in geomorphology and Ruth in climatology. They are also members of the OMF, and for some years they have played a full part both in an agricultural university and in a local church. Here is their testimony of the life they live in a country with very great food needs and a fast-growing population.

*   *   *   *   *

'Who is my neighbour?' The animated discussion went on long past the coffee break and no one even noticed, so intent were they on applying this 2,000-year-old question to their own situation. A group of forty Christian graduates, products of the most prestigious universities in Indonesia, were meeting for a two-day retreat aimed at crystallizing their fluid emotions into solid actions of love and service. Doctors, statisticians, engineers, research scientists and university lecturers were all represented, as well as a crowd of agriculturalists from the university where we teach in Bogor. Many had come to a personal faith in the Lord Jesus Christ during under-graduate days and had grown as disciples of Christ through Bible Study groups on the campus. As students they had learned to study the Word of God for them-selves and to subject their will and reason to His truth. Within the sheltered halls of learning, comforted by a group of like-minded friends and with easy access to a spiritual counsellor, the grass was greener than they ever realized. Only as they emerged to the harsh reality of the outside world, with its conflicting claims and temptations, did they begin to see the need for a deeper understanding of the Gospel.

The opportunities faced by these graduates are limitless and their positions strategic at a national level; if the Church in Indonesia is to fulfil its own great commission at home, it is essential that their vision for Christ and His Kingdom does not fade. The nation faces an uncertain future amidst the struggle for economic development, political stability and self-sufficiency in food production. Its present population of 140 million is growing faster than the available food. The area of derelict land is expanding faster than the area of new land being opened. The vast tracts of virgin forest are rapidly disappearing under the lumberman's saw and the fuel-hungry villager's axe. If the Church is to have any role in the future of the nation it must be able to apply biblical principles to these pressing problems. God has called hundreds of talented Indonesians into the field of agriculture, where they can apply their gifts, their education and above all the love of Christ to the physical and spiritual needs of their own people. Our vision here in Bogor is to see an ever-increasing stream of Christians filling influential leadership positions and there demonstrating the power of Christ in holy living and dedicated service.

Students come to Bogor Agricultural University from all over Indonesia, many from nominally Christian backgrounds but with no personal relationship to Christ. The churches in the traditionally Christian areas are often bound in formality and steeped in animism, so that there is no spiritual life or fellowship, especially for the young people. When they come to Bogor to study they face problems of orientation and culture shock, and the pressure of academic work is compounded by lack of parental supervision, lack of self discipline and crowded living with unsympathetic room mates. The inherited foundations of nominal Christianity crumble under this stress. It is in this context that we have the opportunity of teaching Religious Education to the Protestant freshmen. The foremost tenet of Indonesia's constitution is belief in God, so that religious education is taken seriously and made an integral part of the curriculum of all national education, including the universities. We receive every encouragement and assistance from the Rector in our emphasis on a personal faith which affects morals and conduct, even though he himself is a Muslim.

Although the formal RE class is only for one semester (four months), an informal Campus Fellowship continues the ministry throughout the four years of the agriculture course here. It combines a weekly teaching meeting on the Campus with a network of cell groups which meet for prayer and Bible study in the student residences and lodgings. The leadership training programme is linked with the system of undergraduate teaching assistants, who lead discussions and Bible studies in the RE class and meet each week for a session of preparation, prayer and discipleship training. In this way a core group of 30-40 senior students is given deeper teaching from the Scriptures and the opportunity to exercise pastoral care and oversight of the juniors. During the annual retreat at the end of the RE course, these seniors pass on their training and experience in a programme of workshops and supervised Bible studies.

One of the dangers of an active, loving fellowship in a campus community is that it can draw the students away from their own churches. Yet if these young leaders are to make any permanent impact on their society, it must be through the church. An important part of the programme is therefore to encourage them to be active in the local churches, and this challenge to look beyond their own personal needs and problems and to sacrifice precious time and energy for others is slowly bearing fruit. It is a sign of growing maturity that the campus is represented in almost every youth group and Sunday School in the city.

As the seniors enter their final year they have to spend one long vacation as junior extension officers out in the villages. This is a kind of National Service which is proving extremely valuable. Not only do the students come to realize how little they know, but the Christians learn their own weaknesses when placed in the midst of a non-Christian community. This provides an incentive to learn more about tolerance, witnessing and service within the context of the present society. There are at least six job vacancies for every agriculture student on his graduation, and in the face of many lucrative offers the students already need to have fixed the principles and priorities of seeking the Lord's will. This attitude does not suddenly appear, but develops as the fruit of consistent obedience and faith. Our task here is to prepare them for this vital choice, so that their career is regarded as the Lord's call to missionary service. Some are also beginning to catch the vision of service overseas, especially within countries closed to westerners.

One of the biggest problems in education in Indonesia is the tendency to learn by rote rather than to think deductively. This results in a type of scientist or educationalist who is equipped to maintain the 'status quo' but who cannot pioneer new fields or develop new methods. The emphasis of our academic work at the university here is aimed at teaching the students to think, to ask questions and to draw their own conclusions. At the same time we attempt to train the junior staff members in our respective fields in appropriate teaching methods and research techniques. This research relates especially to the development of new land for agriculture, the preservation of the ecological balance and a deeper understanding of the tropical environment. Thousands of hectares of swamp jungle are being cleared, drained and settled in a large-scale national programme to open up the outer islands of Indonesia by shifting excess population out of Java. The planning of this development involves widespread use of air-photographs for mapping, landscape analysis and survey control. Site selection, clearance and drainage follow as new villages are laid out and the hitherto empty swamp land is prepared for its instant population explosion. In carrying out these surveys, both in the field and in the laboratory, there arise numerous opportunities for teaching not just scientific principles but also the fundamental values of life.

The field of weather and climate as it affects crop growth and food production is relatively new in Indonesia, and it has been necessary to carry out much basic research in order to apply the theories developed in temperate latitudes. An even greater obstacle, however, has been the lack of staff, since there was no undergraduate programme anywhere in the country which catered for this need. Overcoming the inertia and communicating the needs present a constant challenge in the area of personal relationships. Strangely enough, in a country located in the 'wet' tropics, water is the main climatological problem, since the balance between the water available and the requirements of the plants determines the quality of growth. Where new land is being opened up and the settlers are utterly dependent on their own farm produce, it is vital to know which crops will yield successfully during the various seasons of the year. Once again, the principle of training our successors has been foremost in the teaching programme, so that an on-going department with a fully trained staff can prepare the specialists in agro-climatology who are already in demand all over the country.

It is thrilling as we travel around the provincial

universities scattered throughout this 3,000-mile-wide archipelago, to meet graduates from our own classes, now in teaching positions or government research posts. By maintaining communication and passing on new advances we can 'multiply' ourselves and the ministry which God has entrusted to us in an on-going service to the spiritual and physical needs of the country.

10 Truth Spoken and Seen

In so far as the Gospel is the truth of God, neither the oral nor the visible aspects of this truth can be neglected. Jesus during His life on earth said 'I am the Truth'. He said it, He meant it, and He lived it. Men heard the truth from His lips and saw the truth in His life. He spoke at great length and very acceptably. Yet He also manifested the truth by His healing acts, by restoring sight, calming troubled waters, casting out disrupting demons. John's Gospel portrays this perfect balance between word and action, as the discourses of great depth flow around the seven signs worked in the lives and the society of men and women.

His followers showed that they had learnt their lessons well. We see in the Acts of the Apostles that they did not hesitate to use His healing power, and yet they made it crystal clear that it was not by their own power or godliness that they had made a man to walk. The authorities were appalled, not by the healing of the man but by the apostles' obstinate claim that 'It is Jesus' Name and the faith that comes through Him that has given this complete healing to him, as you can all see' (Acts 3.16). No one objects to people being healed, but many protest when that healing is linked with the truth about Jesus Christ. The authorities had seen the truth of the healing, but were quite unwilling to accept the truth of the speaking about Christ. So when they had discussed the whole question, recognizing that the presence of the healed man took away any attempt to deny the visible sign, they could only fall back on a prohibition against speaking any longer to anyone in the Name of Christ. That prohibition the apostles found totally unacceptable. Truth that is seen but not heard is a travesty. 'For we cannot help speaking about what we have seen and heard' (Acts 4.20).

Making the truth seen does not necessarily mean building large institutions or spending large sums of money. Jesus left no institutions behind Him. In the past thirty years, the Gospel has been spreading increasingly around China although large visible Christian activities have been impossible. Yet the Gospel has been seen in countless lives and in many healings that have convinced even hardened opponents that there is truth in Jesus Christ. Some of the activities mentioned in this book are on a small scale. Would that they could spread more widely, but let us not forget that the visibility of Jesus' manifestation of the truth was often limited to a small circle of people.

Truth that is full-orbed must include the whole truth about the whole of humanity. Abraham Maslow in *Motivation and Personality* has helpfully outlined a hierarchy of human needs, beginning with the basic physiological ones, through those of security, social affiliation, recognition and esteem, to self-actualization or fulfilment. At each level the Gospel has something to say that meets those needs at the deepest level. Until the first level of need is met to a basic minimum, a person is little concerned for the other needs; but as each need receives some response, so the interest aspires to further levels. So while it is foolish to preach to a starving man, it is equally foolish to refrain from meeting his greater needs once he has been fed. Furthermore, the Gospel goes beyond the hierarchy developed by Maslow to the deepest need of all, the need for man to have fellowship with the God who made him, opening up to him the prospect of eternal life in all the richness of that term. Without knowing Jesus Christ man's development is stunted. The only way man can come to know God, and Jesus Christ whom He has sent, is through the preaching of the Gospel and response to that truth.

As a missionary fellowship, therefore, we are

unashamed of our calling to speak the truth of Jesus Christ concerning man's needs and God's answers. At the same time, we want that truth to be seen in the lives of those He sends, as also in the lives of those who believe in Him through their word. The visibility of that truth is what this book has been about. We do not profess to have a success story. No doubt we have often made a mess of things, and often missed out on what we should have done. The miracle of mission is not in the little we have seen accomplished, but in the wonder that God can bring any good from the hamfisted fumbling of sinners saved by grace.

More about situations described in this book

Crisis Unawares — Peter Pattisson

Each chapter draws a seed thought or incident from the corresponding chapter of Matthew's Gospel, and illustrates it from the Korean Church today.

Broken Snare — Caroline Stickley

A sometimes luridly frank story carries its readers right into the jungle life of Mindoro, Philippines, to share in the privations, frustrations and increasing success of this missionary venture.

Remember Cambodia — Helen Penfold

The story of the Cambodian Church, its dramatic growth in 1970-1975 and continuing outreach in refugee camps and third world countries.

Dawn Wind

Illustrated with maps, photographs and diagrams, this book tells the story of OMF's work in Thailand over the past 30 years.

Devotional Books from OMF

The Prayer of Faith — J. O. Fraser

The secret of prevailing prayer.

God's Powerful Weapon — Denis Lane

An examination of the teaching and example of Jesus Christ and the apostle Paul about prayer.

Effective Prayer — J. O. Sanders

Brief but pungent studies suggesting some of the principles underlying effective prayer.

Mighty Faith — J. O. Sanders

25 brief meditations challenging the reader to the more effective exercise of faith.

Born for Battle — Arthur Mathews

This book calls not for retreat or going underground at Satan-inspired opposition, but for confrontation.